Housing Management Simplified

Housing Management Simplified

Adelola Dairo

authorHOUSE®

AuthorHouse™ UK
1663 Liberty Drive
Bloomington, IN 47403   USA
www.authorhouse.co.uk
Phone: 0800.197.4150

© 2014 by Adelola Dairo. All rights reserved.

No part of this book may be reproduced, stored in a retrieval system, or transmitted by any means without the written permission of the author.

Published by AuthorHouse   10/28/2014

ISBN: 978-1-4918-8978-7 (sc)
ISBN: 978-1-4918-8979-4 (hc)
ISBN: 978-1-4918-8980-0 (e)

Any people depicted in stock imagery provided by Thinkstock are models, and such images are being used for illustrative purposes only.
Certain stock imagery © Thinkstock.

Because of the dynamic nature of the Internet, any web addresses or links contained in this book may have changed since publication and may no longer be valid. The views expressed in this work are solely those of the author and do not necessarily reflect the views of the publisher, and the publisher hereby disclaims any responsibility for them.

Contents

Chapter One: Introduction to Housing Management 1
- What Is Housing Management? 5
- Two Branches Of Housing Management 7
- General Needs Housing Management 7

Chapter Two: Supported Housing Management................................ 9
- Support Needs... 13
- Keyworking... 15
- Care Plan 20

Chapter Three: General Needs Housing.. 27
- What Is Tenant Participation? 27
- The Importance Of Tenant Participation 29
- Mechanism Of Tenant Participation 31

Chapter Four: Estate Management 33
- What Estate Management Entails... 33
- Estate Inspections... 37
- Estate Agreement 42

Chapter Five: Lettings And Allocations 43

Chapter Six: Rent Collection And Rent Arrears Control 53
- Classification Of Rent Arrears 53
- Rent Arrears Control.. 60
- Procedure For Taking Legal Action 64

Chapter Seven: Anti Social Behaviour 81
- What Constitutes Anti-Social Behaviour? 81
- Who Deals With ASB Cases? 83
- Acceptable Behaviour Contracts 87

- Mediation 94
- Anti-Social Behaviour Orders (ASBOs) 97
- Legal Remedies...101
- Introductory Tenancies...103

Chapter Eight: Tenancy Matters... 115
- Assignment 115
- Succession 118
- Abandonment 121
- Mutual Exchange 123
- Lodgers And Sub-Letting 127
- Ending A Tenancy 130

Chapter Nine: Void Management.. 135
- Causes Of Void 135
- What Constitutes Void Management? 138
- Offering Tenancies And Arranging Viewings 141

Endnotes.. 143
Index.. 145

This manual is a necessity for those working within this sector; providing a breadth of introductory knowledge to Housing Management.

Chapter One

Introduction to Housing Management

INTRODUCTION

To enable us to understand what Housing Management entails, it is important to define a Housing Association.

WHAT IS A HOUSING ASSOCIATION?

A Housing Association is an independent Organisation that exists to provide accommodation for those with housing needs. This is carried out by building new houses and flats and/or by renovating older properties. Housing Associations are mainly non-profit-making Organisations, and are registered as charities. A few are profit making associations established for the purpose of selling "low cost" housing. From April 2012, Housing Associations in England have been funded and regulated by the Homes and Communities Agency (HCA)[1]. This enables them to benefit from public funds.

The body that previously regulated Housing Associations was the Housing Corporation, which was established by the Housing Act 1964. On 1 December 2008, its functions were transferred to two new organisations, the Homes and Communities Agency and the Tenant Services Authority. In 2010, the regulatory role of the Housing Corporation was assigned to a separate body, known as the Tenant Services Authority. However, this role was merged again in April 2012 into the Homes and Communities Agency.[2]

IMPORTANT POINTS

1. Housing Associations are run by Management Committees.

2. These Committees comprise of volunteer members selected due to their relevant professional expertise, or their local knowledge.

3. Tenant representatives are also invited to join the Committees.

4. The Management Committees are legally responsible for the activities of the association and for the effective use of the funds.

5. All members of the committee are prevented by law from deriving any "benefit or privilege".

6. All activities of the registered Housing Associations are monitored and supervised by the Homes and Communities Agencies.

7. The terms 'Registered Social Landlords' or 'Registered Providers' have been used as alternative names for Housing Associations since 2012. 'Registered Social Landlords' is the technical name for social landlords in England who were formerly registered with the Housing Corporation. From 2010 to 2012, Associations were termed 'Registered Providers' under the Housing and Regeneration Act 2008, irrespective of whether they are private, public, for-profit or non-profit making.[3]

HOW ARE HOUSING ASSOCIATIONS FUNDED?

Housing Associations receive their funding from the following main sources:

1. The Homes and Communities Agency

2. Rent and service charges from its occupants

3. Local Authorities

4. Local Government

5. Profit made from private sales

Housing Associations play an important role in Social Housing. Social housing is defined as 'Homes for letting or low cost homeownership, and associated amenities and services, for people whose personal circumstances make it difficult for them to meet their housing needs in the open market'.[4]

Housing Associations and Local Authorities carry out various operations with regards to its properties; this system of operation is known as Housing Management.

TENANCIES USED BY HOUSING ASSOCIATIONS

The type of tenancy also known as Security of Tenure, used by Housing Associations, depends on when the tenancy began. The common types of Agreement used by Housing Associations will certainly fall within one of the following categories:

1. SECURE TENANCY

This includes tenancies created before 15 January 1989 for a self-contained flat or property. This was before the coming into force of the Housing Act 1988. Secure tenancies cannot be issued in the following categories:

- Premises occupied in connection with employment.
- Land acquired for development.
- Temporary accommodation for persons.

2. ASSURED TENANCY

All tenancies on or after 15 January 1989 until 28 February 1997 when the provisions of the Housing Act 1996 in relation to Assured Short-hold Tenancies came into force. In contrast to the secure tenancy it is possible to grant an assured tenancy where the tenant has exclusive possession of a room only and shares other facilities.

It is important to note that even after 28 February 1997 most permanent accommodation granted by housing associations and other housing providers will be assured tenancies and will be described in the tenancy.

3. ASSURED SHORTHOLD TENANCY

This came into place from 28 February 1997 and it was introduced by the Housing Act 1988. The tenancy is initially for a minimum period of 6 months and requires the service of a preliminary notice. Assured short-hold tenancies can be granted on a periodic or fixed term basis.[5]

4. LICENCES

This type of agreement is the most limited of statutory protection and can be ended by the service of a Notice to Quit, without due court process.

WHAT IS HOUSING MANAGEMENT?

There is no specific definition for Housing Management. The activities undertaken to provide lettings or low cost homeownership, with associated amenities and services by Housing Associations, Local Authorities and other housing providers is known as Housing Management.

The following items are thus regarded as Housing Management:

1. Housing management policy formulation.

2. The drawing up of management agreements with voluntary agencies.

3. Tenant selection and transfer, including liaison with referral agencies.

4. Tenancy agreements.

5. Rent setting and collection.

6. Rent recovery.

7. Property insurance.

8. Estate management.

9. Tenant consultation, information and participation related to housing matters only.

10. Dealing with tenant disputes.

11. Giving advice on claiming benefits.

12. Giving advice on debts management in relation to tenancy.

13. Contacting care services.

14. Repairs and maintenance.

15. Care, support and welfare.

TWO BRANCHES OF HOUSING MANAGEMENT

There are two main branches of Housing Management and they include the General Needs Housing Management and the Supported Housing Management.

General needs Housing Management

General needs housing covers the bulk of housing stock for rent. This is stock for which no additional support arrangements have been designated for the residents. It includes self-contained and shared housing.

Sometimes, individual residents of general need properties have specific requirements for additional short or long term management support. Such arrangements are often described as "floating support", but 'temporary' and 'move-on' support may also be delivered using this model. Where such arrangements are in operation the property should be counted within the definition of supported housing.

General needs housing management entails the following:

1. Selection and Allocation - including transfers.

2. Void control.

3. Tenancy Agreements - tenants right.

4. Dealing with evictions.

5. Tenant and service charge collection and arrears control.

6. Repairs and maintenance.

7. Equal opportunities issues in terms of access to housing and other services.

8. Tenant involvement.

Supported Housing entails the following:

1. Housing support
2. Keyworking
3. Care and support

Chapter Two

SUPPORTED HOUSING MANAGEMENT

The definition of supported housing makes a distinction between general needs and supported housing by considering the services being provided, rather than the physical properties of the building.

The term Supported Housing applies where an individual holds a tenancy with an Organisation at the same time as receiving support, including intensive or supportive housing management provided by the Organisation under the terms of a formal undertaking. The three conditions must be met before housing is determined to be supported rather than general needs housing:

1. The Organisation must have a landlord/tenant relationship with the individual receiving the support.

2. The level of housing support provided must be over and above that which the Organisation would generally provide for general needs housing.

3. The Organisation must have formally accepted responsibility for providing the housing and related support to the residents, either directly or indirectly through a formal relationship with another organisation or voluntary body.

Supported housing caters for a wide range of client groups with a need for different levels of support in shared and self-contained accommodation.

FUNDING SUPPORTED HOUSING

Supported Housing was largely developed under the Housing Corporation's special needs framework. In addition, a significant proportion of schemes have been funded by Health Authorities, Local Authorities and Charities. With supported housing projects, care or support services and revenue funding can come from a variety of sources, depending on who is housed.

THE ROLE OF SUPPORTED HOUSING SCHEMES

The role of the schemes is to provide support, either on a permanent or temporary basis, to enable people to maintain accommodation appropriate to their needs. This aspect of housing expanded considerably during the 1970's and 1980's mainly due to policy changes in two key areas:

1. The closure of large institutions for people with mental health problems and learning disabilities.

2. Government initiatives with regards to housing homeless people.

The underlying philosophy of most supported provision is that services are best provided in small community settings rather than in large institutional settings. This philosophy has been reinforced by the growth of community care, with the recognition that supported housing can be provided for people with support needs in self-contained and shared housing provision.

However, there is recognition that it is not always possible to provide services to people in their existing homes. In certain circumstances some people require specialist provision in supported housing schemes, for example:

1. People who are homeless and need support to enable them to live independently.

2. People who live with careers and are unable to cope.

3. People excluded from their homes due to violence, sexual abuse, relationship breakdown, harassment or abuse.

4. People who require specially adapted accommodation and support because of their mobility and health problems.

5. People requiring a level of care and support that would be too expensive to provide in their own home.

TYPES OF SUPPORTED HOUSING SCHEMES

1. Short Stay

This aims at dealing with an immediate crisis such as exclusion, abuse, violence, harassment, and homelessness.

2. Temporary stay

This includes schemes that assist people move towards independent living. There is emphasis on the development of independent life skills or rehabilitation and assistance in obtaining permanent re-housing with reduced or no support. One example of this is a hostel.

3. Permanent stay

These are schemes that provide long-term support in certain circumstances because of e.g. disabilities, frailty, and health problems. Examples of such schemes include the Residential Care homes and sheltered schemes.

NEED GROUPS HOUSED

The groups of people for whom Supported Housing can be provided for and who are eligible for special needs funding are mainly:

- People with mental health problems.

- People with learning difficulties.

- Young people at risk or leaving care.
- Frail elderly people.
- People with physical disabilities.
- People with alcohol or drug problems.
- Women at risk of domestic violence.
- Single homeless people.
- Refugees.
- People leaving penal establishment or at risk of offending.
- People with HIV or Aids.

Supported housing providers have used the generic term "single homeless people" to describe their client group to avoid labelling.

SERVICES PROVIDED IN SUPPORTED HOUSING

The services provided under supported housing are:

1. Intensive Housing Management.
2. Housing services.
3. Personal services.
4. Care and support.

INTENSIVE HOUSING MANAGEMENT

This is an extension of regular general needs housing management which involves extra support around activities or skills that are needed to cope with managing a tenancy agreement. This includes support with regards the following:

1. Welfare benefit advice and support.

2. Resettlement also known as 'move-on'.

3. Advice on housing matters.

4. Accessing other services.

5. Informal counselling.

SUPPORT NEEDS

The focus will be on single homeless people, their needs can be diverse and varied and they include the following:

1. Housing needs:

While there is obviously a need for shelter, there is also a need for housing that is appropriate in design, location and available amenities. Housing should also be relatively comfortable and safe.

2. Support needs:

This includes health care needs and assistance with physical tasks and the organisation of one's life. It also includes welfare rights services.

3. Daily living skills:

Some single homeless people may need life skill training to learn how to manage a home and also money.

4. Money Management skills:

Single homelessness is strongly associated with relatively low incomes, thus require assistance in managing their income.

5. Social needs:

There is evidence that some single homeless people may not have social and emotional relationships. This is because isolation and boredom contribute to an inability to live successfully in permanent accommodation. While some single homeless people have very profound levels of need in all these areas, others have only limited support needs besides their housing need. Some single homeless people have no needs other than their housing needs.

KEYWORKING

WHAT IS KEYWORKING?

A keyworker is a named worker who is responsible for co-ordinating the support needs of an individual client. The extent of support will vary between individuals and the setting. It is a professional relationship and the keyworker is responsible for establishing and maintaining boundaries and ensuring that the key client understands the limits of confidentiality. Ultimately, keyworking is about providing a safe environment in which the client can explore, learn, grow and progress into independent living.

REASONS FOR A KEYWORKER SYSTEM

1. The named keyworker is known to the client, family, friends and other professionals and will normally be able to provide a "one stop" service.

2. Client needs are more likely to be identified and met.

3. They provide individual opportunities for 1 to 1 quality time.

4. They are an internal advocate for the client.

5. They provide continuity of care and clarity about who's doing what. Issues are followed up and relevant records are maintained.

6   It provides motivation and quality assurance to the client.

7   It helps to share workload among the team and define areas of responsibility.

KEYWORKING INVOLVES

1. Planning and problem solving.

2. Employment and advocacy.

3. Providing access to service and stimulating activity.

4. Ensuring opportunities for participation and fulfilment.

5. Creating a sense of purpose and change.

6. Good listening and communication skills.

7. Understanding and maintaining confidentiality.

8. Promoting independence.

9. Needs assessment.

10. Working in a client-centred approach and genuineness.

11. Being non-judgmental.

12. Supporting others to take risks and make mistakes.

13. Maintaining accurate and legible records.

14. Supporting clients and service users.

KEYWORKER'S CHECK LIST

1. **Establishing the Relationship.**

   - Introducing self and explaining the role of a keyworker.

   - Discussing previous experience of keyworking.

   - Establishing boundaries by discussing the expectations of both parties.

   - Explaining the limits of confidentiality, access to records and information.

- Agreeing when and where you will meet, how long for and how often.

- Explaining the complaints procedure.

- Formalising the above points into verbal or written agreement.

2. **Maintaining the Relationship.**

   - Assessing the client's needs.

   - Agreeing goals with the client.

   - Plan how the goals are to be achieved.

   - Putting goals and plans into action and monitoring their progress.

   - Regular reviews of the relationship.

   - Evaluating and reviewing goals, and also praising, rewarding and celebrating achieved goals.

   - Defining new goals.

3. **Ending the Relationship**

   - Reviewing progress and the relationship.

   - Highlighting the good and bad times in the relationship.

   - Discussing the end of the relationship, why it is ending, who will take over.

   - Prepare client for new Keyworker.

   - Marking the end of the relationship with a gesture.

CONFIDENTIALITY

Confidentiality is vital in Keyworking in order to avoid difficulties in the relationship. There is a fine line between confidentiality, secrecy and collusion.

1. Confidentiality is information, which is given from one party to another, and should not be shared with a third party unless there is a good reason for the third party to know that information.
2. Secrecy is where the two parties keep information to themselves, even though, there is a good reason for a third party to know it.
3. Collusion is the natural extension of secrecy, i.e. acting on the basis of the secret information, even though this may be harmful to self or to others.

In Social Care work the keyworker operates within an Organisational structure. Their job is to ensure that the best possible service is provided to the clients. They are accountable to the line manager and they work as a representative of the team.

KEYWORKING IN THE COMMUNITY

The role of a keyworker in the community are as follows:

1. Providing access to services.
2. Making services sensitive to different communities.
3. Developing skills of service users.
4. Establishing eligibility to services.
5. Protecting the rights of service users.
6. Advocating for claims to service by users.
7. Making care plans.
8. Connecting people to services.
9. Linking service providers.
10. Solving the Organisation's network problems.
11. Ensuring service delivery.
12. Monitoring quality of service.
13. Supporting service users, their families and friends.
14. Stimulating activities and new services.

CARE PLAN

A Care Plan is also known as a service plan or treatment plan and it is defined as follows:

1. Plan of professional clinical activities developed to implement the treatment plan.

2. A written document that outlines the types and frequency of the long-term care services that a person receives.

3. It is a written statement developed for an entitled person/s which states the nursing and other interventions to be undertaken, the health outcomes to be achieved and the review of care which will occur at regular intervals.

4. Each person has a care plan which describes the current care arrangements. The plan is reviewed after 28 days, three months and six months thereafter.

5. The care plan has Health and Education (Personal Education Plan) components and describes the contact arrangements between the young person and his/her birth family.

SKILLS AND KNOWLEDGE NEEDED FOR CARE PLANNING

1. Keywork training.

2. Knowledge and understanding of the client group.

3. Good communication skills.

4. Report writing skills.

5. Listening skills.

6. Understanding of anti-discriminatory practice.

Housing Management Simplified

7. Understanding the limits of confidentiality.

8. Understand the links between keyworking and supervision.

9. Ability to empathize with the client.

10. Knowledge of local resources.

11. Ability to form relationships with other professionals.

12. Knowledge of relevant legislation.

THE CARE PLANNING PROCESS

STAGES IN THE PROCESS

1. Assessment
2. Goal Setting
3. Action Planning
4. Implementation
5. Review

THE PROCESS IS ONGOING:

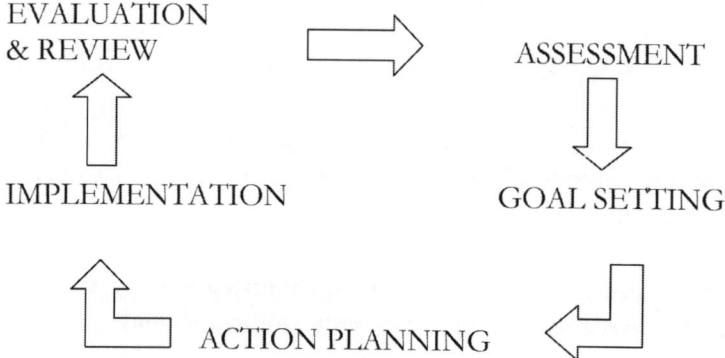

STAGE ONE

ASSESSMENT

Assessment can be divided into two sections, Information Gathering and Need Assessment. Information gathering is the stage of absorbing all available information about a client, in order to make a need assessment. Sources of this information include:

1. The client

2. The client's family/friends

3. Previous keyworker

4. Other professionals such as Social Worker, General Practitioner etc.

This information can be gathered from the following sources:

1. Observation

2. Referral form

3. Attending client's review

4. Interviews and meetings

5. Written records and reports

6. Conversation

During the information gathering stage you merely absorb the information without processing or starting to assess. This has to be carried out sensitively and with empathy.

Once you have gathered all the relevant information you will be ready to make a needs assessment. Two staff workers should carry out this assessment rather than one individual, to ensure that one person does not impose their views and beliefs on the client.

STAGE TWO

GOAL SETTING

Having assessed a client's needs, based on the information available and a specific assessment model, you can now set goals. These goals must meet the needs of the clients as well as reflect current values. Goals should include the following:

1. DIGINITY needs to be protected at all times and goals should aim to safe guard client's self-respect.

2. RIGHTS to live freely as other members of the community, should be reflected in the goals set.

3. CHOICE is only valid if the client has real options and understands those options.

4. PRIVACY should not be impinged on by goals set, and clients should have the right to privacy whenever they want it.

5. INDEPENDENCE goals should help the client live an independent life.

6. FULFILLMENT goals should enable clients to achieve their potential in all areas of assessment.

Goal should be divided into Short, Medium and Long Term Goals and one should only work on a few goals at a time.

Set S.M.A.R.T Goals

1. SPECIFIC

2. MEASURABLE

3. ACHIEVABLE

4. REALISTIC

5. TIME-LIMITED

STAGE THREE

ACTION PLANNING

To achieve successful goals, there needs to be a plan. The following factors need to be taken into consideration:

1. Who will do what, where, and when?

2. Does the goal need assessing for risk?

3. Is the client motivated?

4. Do we have sufficient staffing levels?

5. Is the team motivated to support the client?

6. What resources are available?

7. What is the current mental and physical health of the client?

STAGE FOUR

IMPLEMENTATION

This is a very important stage where things often go wrong; one reason for this may be due to the lack of monitoring of the plan once it is put in to action. At this stage the keyworker needs to use their observation skills as well as their communication skills.

The following issues need to be considered:

1. Is the plan working, does it need amending?

2. Is the client enjoying himself or herself?

3. Is it causing stress to the client?

4. Do we need to review the original goal?

5. Are all staff following the plan consistently?

6. Do the staff members understand the plan?

7. Is the client benefitting from the plan?

It is very important that the Care Plan be closely monitored. If the plan is not working there's little or no point in continuing it. Maybe something is missing in the plan, or perhaps the goal was not appropriated. Where the needs assessed accurately? Did they have the right information in place?

STAGE FIVE

REVIEW

The Care Plan can be reviewed at any time, especially if you do not think it is working. We recommend you review the Care Plan with your client at least every six months. Ask your client how they think it's going. This is time to celebrate successes and achievements, as well as recognize where things may have gone wrong. Reviewing the Care Plan means reviewing the services available to the client, the practice set in place and the client's progress.

The following questions may also have to be considered:

1. Was the client offered enough support?

2. What worked well?

3. What did not work?

4. What would we do differently?

5. Did we have the correct information?

6. Where do we go from here?

Reviewing the Care Plan involves starting the process again to gather the information required to draw up a needs assessment and set goals for the coming period of time.

Care plans have to be a life document that is referred to frequently, is easily accessible and well understood by all staff involved in the support of the individual client.

Chapter Three

GENERAL NEEDS HOUSING

The following areas will be covered under the General Needs Housing: Tenant Participation, Estate Management, Lettings and Allocation, Rent Collection and Rent Arrears Control, Anti-social Behaviour Management, Tenancy Matters and Void Management. This information should provide a broad knowledge of what Housing Management entails.

TENANT PARTICIPATION

WHAT IS TENANT PARTICIPATION?

Participation means 'to share in'. This means tenants/residents having a share in the decisions with regards to their housing. It is a legal obligation that tenants be informed or consulted with and that they can register their opinions on proposals. The Council /Housing Associations are obliged to consider their comments. This is in accordance with the Housing Acts of 1988 and 1989.

The three main types of Participation:

1. Consultation

2. Involvement

3. Control

CONSULTATION

To consult means 'to seek the view of or advice from'. It also means 'to seek permission or the opinion of'. The council and social landlords seek the opinion of their tenants with regards to the services provided to them and proposals.

Methods of consultation

Communication is vital between Tenants and the Housing Providers, it is important that communication channels are well structured and in place, thereby creating a room for dialogue. Listening is just as important; the council must listen to what the people are saying. This enables them to work together.

The various mechanisms that can be developed for this purpose are thus:

1. Tenant Newsletters
2. Satisfaction Surveys
3. Questionnaires
4. Suggestion Box
5. Structured complaints procedure
6. Tenant Meetings

INVOLVEMENT

To involve means 'to include as a necessary part or result'. This means that tenants are involved right from the beginning with decisions with regards to their housing and proposals that may concern them. This also occurs when tenants are members of the various bodies that make decisions.

CONTROL

The word Control means 'the power to influence people's behaviour, or the course of events'. This means tenants having control of decisions; facilities and resources; thereby enabling them to influence the future of their estate.

THE IMPORTANCE OF TENANT PARTICIPATION

1. It serves as a means of ensuring that quality services are provided which are tailored to meet the needs of the tenants.

2. It enhances good decision-making. This is because tenants have better knowledge of their estates and the services they require.

3. This results in greater commitment; from tenants to follow proposals through and from the Organisation to deliver these services.

4. There is a sense of achievement for the tenants, also their skills and talents are put to use, new skills are gained, and the self-esteem of the tenants is improved.

5. It improves working relationships between the Housing Providers and their tenants.

AIMS OF TENANT PARTICIPATION

1. To review and improve the quality of services provided.

2. To reach minority groups such as ethnic groups, women, young people, etc. To also get them involved.

3. To organize priorities and address them according to tenant's recommendation.

4. To develop services required by tenants.

5. To set up an Organisation and other constituted bodies.

6. To plan the budget for the property or estate.

7. To set up a good feedback system on the services provided.

MECHANISM OF TENANT PARTICIPATION

Working Parties: Whereby staffs from the council and Housing Association and tenants put heads together and look into ways of tackling existing issues.

Tenant Representatives: Whereby tenants represent the voice of the people with regards to various proposals put forward.

Tenant Association: These are voluntary groups of Tenants that aim to provide social and community events and services; They act on behalf of tenants as pressure groups on the Local Authority to put the opinion of the tenant forward.

Estate Forums: Similar to working parties, they include tenants, leaseholders, and local council workers that meet together to discuss problems regarding the estate and look into ways of addressing them.

Focus Groups: This involves selecting 8-10 people on an estate to work with you in addressing a specific issue on the estate. They would represent the views of the estate and once that project is completed the group is dissolved. This is very useful in drawing up Neighbourhood Agreement on an estate. The group should represent the ethnic mix on the estate.

Tenant Meeting: The tenants and the management team meet to discuss various issues and proposals. They voice their concerns and views to the team, which is put into consideration during decision making.

Chapter Four

ESTATE MANAGEMENT

What Estate Management entails

This is the continuous management of the cleaning services provided on an Estate by the Estate-based staff members. As well as the activities mentioned below, Estate Management also seeks to highlight issues particular to a specific Estate, with the aim of addressing the problem.

The most effective way to achieve this is by the use of Estate Inspections. This inspection is carried out by the Housing Managers, Tenants/Residents, Caretakers and Contractors. It uses target settings and measurements to raise the environmental standard of the Estate.

Estate Management entails the following:

1. Cleaning services

2. Gardening

3. The removal of abandoned vehicles

4. Carrying out repairs

5. Addressing Antis Social Behaviour (ASB) issues

6. Regeneration

7. Development

8. Other activities such as Parking management and Garage/ Bike shed control

CLEANING SERVICES

There should be a set standard in place for the cleaning of the communal areas to ensure that a high standard of service is provided and that residents are provided with a pleasant environment to live in. Residents should be consulted about service standards for their block or estate and they should be given a real say in the determination of both the quality and the cost.

Residents' comments on the service provided should be welcomed by Social Landlords. Prompt action needs to be taken to improve the service provided to residents whenever this falls below acceptable standards.

GARDENING

This service can either be maintained in-house or by contractors. Where this is maintained by Estate-based staff such as Caretakers, it is important that the Housing Officer maintains an inventory of the tools available. He/she should also ensure that staff are adequately trained on the use of these tools.

The following should also be in place:

1. If materials or tools are to be stored on the estate, then secure premises must be established.

2. Any dangerous chemicals must be kept in a locked cabinet, with adequate ventilation or fire protection where appropriate.

3. A proper tool rack must be in place. This must be capable of supporting each tool independently and safely, and compartments for tools should be clearly labelled.

4. Tools must be returned to the rack after use.

5. Tools should be properly maintained in accordance with manufacturer's instructions.

6. All electrical equipment must be checked annually and certified as safe by a qualified technician.

7. A formal inspection of the tools should be carried out every three months and the results noted on the Estate Inspection Form.

Where the services are provided by a Gardening Contractor, a Service Level Agreement must be in place. This clearly sets out the details of the service that will be provided and service standards required. It is vital that residents are involved in the drawing up of the contract. The contractors will be required to attend the inspections to obtain feedback regarding their service, and be informed about any areas of concern and look for ways of resolving them. They will also get to know their customers.

REMOVAL OF ABANDONED VEHICLES

It is very important that Social Landlords have set procedures and policies to deal with the removal of all abandoned vehicles. Such vehicles include untaxed vehicles, vehicles that are not road worthy and unsafe vehicles which may pose a potential danger to the residents on the estate.

Every local authority has a statutory duty to remove vehicles which are a danger to public health or the environment. Where the vehicle is on private land, the local authority will not do anything without a request in writing giving them consent to enter that land. In the absence of a specific request form being supplied, a letter requesting that the Local Authority removes the vehicle will suffice.

CARRYING OUT REPAIRS

It is very important that inspections are carried out on the Estate. This highlights any health and safety issues; locates outstanding repairs and ensures that they are addressed within the required time limit.

Examples of repairs that you should watch out for includes:

1. The internal lights
2. Entrance doors
3. External lights
4. Blocked drainage
5. Lifts
6. Entry door system

Social landlords should either employ a contractor to deal with the major repairs and closely monitor the service provided.

ADDRESSING ASB ISSUES

This is one of the quickest ways to obtain information on anti social behaviour taking place on an estate. Residents will inform the estate based staff members of such behaviour. Evidence of continuous graffiti on the walls, broken windows and other damages may also highlight the existence of such problems on the Estate.

It is very important that a plan of immediate action is in place to address these problems as they arise. The Police and other external agencies may be consulted to assist in addressing the problem.

ESTATE INSPECTIONS

It is important to ensure that the environment of an estate is kept clean and tidy to create a community where people desire to live. Estate inspection is a useful tool to achieve this purpose and enables you to measure the improvements made on a particular scheme.

WHO ATTENDS THE INSPECTION?

1. The Housing Manager
2. Residents on the scheme
3. Surveyor or repair inspector
4. Estate-based staff such as caretakers, cleaners or handyman

WHAT DOES THE INSPECTION COVER?

1. All communal areas.
2. The exterior of the estate
3. The car parks
4. The grounds
5. The general standard of services provided on that estate

THE IMPORTANCE OF ESTATE INSPECTION

1. To raise the standard of the services provided on the estate.
2. To involve tenants/residents in the management process.
3. To demonstrate customer care.

4. To highlight issues specific to the estate and help set targets to ensure that they are addressed accordingly.

5. To inform staff of tenants/residents priorities.

6. To strengthen the partnership between residents and the organisation providing the services to them.

7. To help staff members record and monitor progress and manage the performance of the repairs contractor.

THE PROCESS

1. Identify the estate and set a date for the first inspections. This should be carried out every 4-6 weeks.

2. Send out letters to all tenants/residents living on the estate, explaining the process and asking them to attend. A minimum of one and a maximum of five residents per inspection are sufficient.

3. Carry out the first inspection. There should be a scoring process from 1-20, with a bench-mark of either 14 or 15 where standards are maintained.

4. The residents should be involved in the scoring process, while the Housing Manager notes all the highlighted issues. Targets and completion dates should be set for these issues to be addressed and resolved.

5. Copies of the inspection sheets should be available to all residents upon request.

6. The Housing Manager should ensure that all highlighted issues are addressed accordingly and an estate agreement is drawn, giving a period of one year to address three of the main issues of tenants/residents.

7. There should be continuous monitoring of performance and progress.

Housing Management Simplified

ESTATE INSPECTION REPORT

ESTATE NAME	INSPECTED BY	DATE

Item number	Service provided/ Area inspected	Comments/ action required	Action By who?	Target date for completion	Score 1-20
1	Entrance Halls, Stairways, doors & Springs				
2	Communal Rooms				
3	Communal Windows				
4	Internal Lighting				
5	Litter Internal				
6	Evidence of graffiti?				
7	Car Parks				
8	Courtyards & Footpath				
9	External Lighting				
10	Exterior Paintwork				
11	Estate Signs				
12	External Repairs Required				
13	Health & Safety Issues				
14	Boundary Walls & Fences				
15	Refuse Bin Area				

16	Litter External				
17	Communal Gardens				
18	Grassed Areas				
19	Hedges & Trees				
20	Resident Gardens				
21	Drains & Gutters				
22	Noticeboards				
23	Abandoned & Untaxed Vehicles				
24	Lifts				
				Total Score	
				Average Score	

1	2	3	4	5	6	7	8	9	10	11	12	13	14	15	16	17	18	19	20

(1-4 =Very poor)   (5 = Poor)   (14-16 Satisfactory)   (17-20 Exceptional)

Date of previous Inspection		Previous Inspection Average score	
Date of next Inspection		Target for next Inspection	
Signature of Officer Inspecting		Date	
Signature of Resident Inspecting		Date	
Signature of Resident Inspecting		Date	

ESTATE INSPECTION REPORT: ITEMS TO BE ADDRESSED

ESTATE NAME	INSPECTED BY	DATE

Item Number	Service provided/ Area inspected	Comments/ Action required	Actioned by who	Target for completion

ESTATE AGREEMENT

The Local Authorities and Social Landlords come into agreement with their clients to deliver specific services over a period of time on an estate. This process is known as an Estate Agreement and the duration is over a period of one year, after which it is reviewed.

IMPORTANCE OF ESTATE AGREEMENT

The Estate Agreement is a tool to ensure that the Organisation/Local Authority get things done. They:

1. Help re-shape services provided.
2. Demonstrate customer care.
3. Enhance residents' participation.
4. Build partnership.
5. Enhance accountability.
6. Improves the quality of services.

WHAT ESTATE AGREEMENT ENTAILS

It involves information gathering through tenant surveys and other mechanisms, to establish what the current issues are on the estate. Through the formation of residents' focus groups or residents meeting, the social landlords are able to come into dialogue with their residents to establish the priorities on the estate. Both parties agree on the issues to be addressed over a period of one year. The focus should not be on more than 2-4 issues, to ensure appropriate monitoring.

This is drawn up as an agreement between the housing provider and that estate. It is signed and dated by the resident's representatives and the housing manager. The agreement has to be reviewed every six months, as the needs of the tenant can change and new issues that require immediate attention can arise.

Chapter Five

LETTINGS AND ALLOCATIONS

This deals with the process of deciding whom to offer a vacant property to, how to offer a property and carry out the letting to meet the needs of the people. It includes meeting the needs of existing customers as well as housing new applicants.

All housing providers are required to allocate their properties to meet the housing needs in line with the Government's Housing Strategy. They are required to ensure that they are making a positive contribution to their communities and that their clients are happy with the properties offered to them.

Housing Associations are required to:

1. Work in partnership with the local authorities to meet the local housing needs.

2. Create sustainable local communities which are successful.

3. Ensure that all vacant properties are let quickly within a minimum turnaround period.

4. Ensure that people are housed in accommodations that meet their housing requirements.

HOUSING NEW APPLICANTS

The allocation options for new applicants also referred to as external applicants are as follows:

1. Local Authority Nominations

2. Referral Agencies

3. Direct Applications

4. Local Initiatives

HOUSING EXISTING CUSTOMERS

The allocation options for existing customers who are also referred to as internal applications are:

1. Transfers

2. Mutual Exchange

3. Purchase Options

TRANSFERS

Local Authorities and Social Landlords should ensure that a reasonable proportion of their Letting stock is made available to meet the needs of their existing customers. This is operated by a waiting list process in the order of priority needs.

The various types of needs are as follows:

1. Overcrowding

2. Medical Grounds

3. Decant

4. Harassment

5. Under-occupation

OVERCROWDING

This is when the number of permanent members of a household has increased and the house is now too small. There is a standard size of accommodations offered to people, when the current tenant exceeds that size; it is usually the obligation of their landlord to put them in suitable accommodations.

The general number of person per size accommodations are as follows:

1. One bed flat or a room in a shared property or a bedsit - This is offered to a single person.

2. One bed room accommodation - This will be offered to a couple

3. Two bedroom flat - This can either be offered to a single person/couple with one child, or two children of the same sex, or of different sexes if they are under the age of eight years.

4. Three bedroom flat - This will be offered to a single person/couple with three children or two children of different sexes with the eldest over eight years old, or two children of the same sex with an age gap of 15 years or more.

5. Four bedroom flat - This will be offered to a couple or a single person with four or more children depending on their ages and sex.

MEDICAL GROUNDS

This is when the medical condition of a member of the household makes the current property no longer suitable for the family. Documented evidence will have to be provided to support the application, such as a medical report.

DECANT

This is when repair works need to be carried to a tenanted property and the works cannot be carried out while the household is in occupation. The landlord has an obligation to re-house the family, either on a temporary bases until the works have been completed, or re-house them on a permanent bases. This also covers refurbishment.

HARASSMENT

When a household is suffering serious harassment issues which cannot be resolved efficiently by means other than a transfer, the landlord is obligated to provide alternative accommodation to the household. Examples of harassment cases include both racial and sexual harassment, and other anti-social behaviour cases that render the household unsafe in their existing property.

UNDER-OCCUPATION

This is when the home is larger than the need of the household. Housing providers usually promote this by offering a financial incentive and assistance with the move. The amount of the incentive depends on the number of rooms the tenant will be giving up. The tenant will be offered a property, which meets the needs of his or her household.

MUTUAL EXCHANGE

A Mutual exchange is the process whereby two or more existing tenants move into each other's house. Each resident takes on the tenancy agreement of the property they are moving into. An exchange may be between the same Landlord or two different Landlords. This enables residents to be more suitably housed in a property of their choice at little or no cost to the landlords.

Assured and Secured tenants have legal rights to Mutual Exchange, however, the application has to be approved by the Landlord/s and they may refuse to proceed with the exchange based on their policies.

DECANTING

Introduction

Decanting is the process by which tenanted properties are vacated to allow conversions, improvements, major repairs or maintenance works to be carried out. A decant is necessary when the works are so extensive or disruptive that it would be unreasonable for the tenants to live in the property whilst work is undertaken. Decants can either be permanent or temporary depending on the nature of the work proposed. It is the responsibility of the Housing provider to determine the type of decants to be operated. Housing Associations and the Local Authorities use permanent decants only if it is absolutely necessary; due to the cost of the works carried out.

A permanent decant is usually considered for the following types of works, however, the decision has to be made in consultation with the landlord and the resident. They include thus:

1. Major repairs

2. Conversions

3. Improvements

MAJOR REPAIRS

This covers extensive work to one or more major structural elements of the property. For instance, roof, wall, or damp repair work to a majority of the property. Work will usually take between one to twelve weeks, and the tenant will be moved as either a permanent or temporary decant. It is appropriate to offer permanent decant to reduce the level of discomfort to the household. Social providers should have policies in place that details the procedures.

CONVERSIONS

This is the process of developing run down properties which require massive refurbishment. It also includes conversion of units of properties for the first time such as a conversion from bedsit units into one bed flats. In such cases the tenants will be permanently decanted.

IMPROVEMENTS

This involves modernisation and full refurbishment to a block of properties. The improvement works usually take nine months and above and permanent decant will be required.

TEMPORARY DECANT

A temporary decant is carried out when a property requires maintenance work which is less extensive but cannot be carried out with the household in situ. Examples of such works include the treatment of mould and sound proofing. Housing Management will refer such properties to the surveyor to determine the works proposed, the risks involved with tenants being around while the work is in process and the length of time it will take to complete the whole work.

This will be discussed with the tenant and the decision usually made is to re-house the tenant temporarily while the problems in the property are addressed. Various options need to be discussed with the tenant such as moving in with friends, or staying in a bed and breakfast or a ready to let void. The best option should be offered.

The following need to be addressed by Housing Management:

1. **Payment to tenant**

The landlord has to pay the tenant all the costs incurred during the process of moving, as well as the inconveniences caused as a result of moving. The following are examples of costs that need to be covered are disturbance allowance, removal cost, storage cost (if applicable), connection and disconnection cost, postal redirection cost, travel cost and other costs as necessary.

2. Rent Account

The tenant's account details will have to be updated with respect to the temporary decant for legal purposes. The tenant is required to continue paying the rent on their usual address at the usual rate, via their normal method of payment, whether this be rent card, bank payment or standing order.

3. Housing Benefit

If a tenant is claiming Housing Benefit, the landlord will write to the appropriate Housing Benefit Office explaining that the tenant has been temporarily decanted, with dates. They have to explain that the tenant is still liable for the rent on their normal address, at the usual rate. The claim should be continuous and the tenant should not have to make a fresh application for Housing Benefit, unless requested to do so by the Housing Benefit department, for instance, if the claim is in a renewal period.

It is the responsibility of the landlord to keep the tenant updated on the progress of works, this includes informing them as to what stage the repair works are at, and when they will be in a position to return to their home. On completion of the works, Housing Management will immediately inform the tenant and agree on a date to move back into the property.

PERMANENT DECANTS

Due to the cost of permanent decants they should only be considered if absolutely necessary due to nature of the work. Where the tenant can move back into the property following works then temporary decants should be the norm.

Where the works are such that the tenant has to move permanently because the nature of the property is to be altered, or where the works are extensive improvement works, the Housing Manager in consultation with the tenant can decide on a permanent decant. The Housing Officer will carry out an assessment of the tenant's housing needs and pass this information to the Housing Manager.

The Housing Manager will have to take full account of the tenant's essential housing requirements as they will be moved on a permanent basis. Once an assessment has been carried out, offers are made to the tenant.

The tenant is usually made two offers before progressing the case to court, however this will be dependent on how urgent the possession of the property is, and how likely it is that a suitable property will become available for offer to the tenant, given the restrictions of some essential requirements.

The individual circumstances of each case will be taken into consideration, and the housing manager will discuss with the solicitor whether Court action is necessary. A Notice of Seeking Possession may be served at this point. What action can be taken depends on the nature of the works to be carried out.

PAYMENT TO TENANTS

Permanent decants are much more expensive to Landlords because they have to pay out more to their customers. They are required to make a home loss payment, which may cost from £1,500 to £3,500 per tenant depending on the Organisation. They are to make other payments such as cost on soft furnishing payments, disturbance allowance, removal cost, disconnection and reconnection cost and other cost.

The housing Officer is responsible for ensuring that all necessary arrangements are in place to enable the tenant to move to a permanent new home, ensuring that they receive the home-loss payment, and that other costs are reimbursed as quickly as possible.

RENT ACCOUNT

The rent account for the existing tenancy has to be ended, and a new tenancy created for the new property. The tenant will have to sign a new document and complete all the usual forms in the Organisation's sign-up pack, giving usual advice on rents, amenities, and welfare rights like all new tenants.

HOUSING BENEFIT

For all permanent decant the tenant is required to fill a new housing benefit form with a letter from their Housing Manager explaining the reason for the move. This should also include a copy of the new tenancy agreement for the new address.

Chapter Six

RENT COLLECTION AND RENT ARREARS CONTROL

DEFINITION OF RENT ARREARS

Rent arrears can be defined as the debts attached to any household that are behind with their rent payments. This also includes service charges payments.

CLASSIFICATION OF RENT ARREARS

1. Housing Benefit Arrears

2. Personal

3. Social Services

HOUSING BENEFIT ARREARS

These are arrears due to tenants awaiting a decision on their Housing Benefit entitlement. One has to be careful when determining if arrears should be categorized under Housing Benefit or not. The following criteria can be used when classifying Housing Benefit arrears.

1. The Housing Benefit application form was submitted and proof of submission must be on record. (Only for tenants on State Benefits)

2. All necessary documents required by Housing Benefit were submitted to Housing Benefit with proof and receipt.

3. Housing Benefit must be under four weeks from the date the application form was submitted.

4. Housing Benefit has notified that the claim will be put in interim payment.

5. Arrears can only be classified under Housing Benefit when it is longer than four weeks. This is only under the condition that Housing Benefit has confirmed in writing that arrears will be backdated from the date of benefit application. Housing Benefit must also confirm the date when payment will be made.

6. All underpayments are confirmed in writing and the period of underpayment is clearly stated by Housing Benefit.

7. Arrears Recovery staff can also use their initiative in determining who is responsible for arrears.

PERSONAL ARREARS

Personal arrears is rent due from the tenant personally, either by way of contributing to their rent after receiving Housing Benefit support, or if they are fully responsible for the full rent.

It should be noted that all tenants are likely to fall under the category of personal arrears as Housing Benefit may not pay for the service charges.

HOW DO YOU DETERMINE PERSONAL ARREARS?

1. Tenants with no rent rebate assistance from Housing Benefit.

2. Working tenants on a high income with irregular payment patterns.

3. Working Tenants on Low income but earning above the applicable amount.

4. Tenants with no proof of applying for Housing Benefit but have provided all of the necessary documents required by Housing Benefit.

5. Tenants that their Housing Benefit was not paid after four weeks of making an application.

6. The repayment of overpayments: Housing Benefit can request that tenants repay all overpayments. It is very important to adjust any amount of overpayment directly to the personal rent account and inform the tenant immediately of the change and subsequent rent liability.

7. Tenants who receive their Housing Benefit directly from the Organisation but have no control over liaison on their behalf with Housing Benefit.

8. Tenants whose Housing Benefit was stopped for any reason. They should be made liable for their rent immediately their benefit was stopped and immediate information should be relayed to tenants.

UNIVERSAL CREDIT SYSTEM

It is very important to note at this stage that the Universal Credit System was introduced in April 2013 and will be implemented from October 2013. Universal Credit is a new simpler, single monthly payment for people in or out of work, which merges together some of the benefits and tax credit that the person might be receiving.[6]

Universal Credit will replace:

1. Income-based Jobseeker's Allowance

2. Income-related Employment and Support Allowance

3. Income Support

4. Child Tax Credit

5. Working Tax Credit

6. Housing Benefit

Universal Credit will be paid monthly into the claimant's account. If the claimant gets help with their rent, this will be included in the monthly payment - they will be required to pay the landlord themselves. For a couple, a monthly payment will be paid for the household and they will be required to pay their landlord.

Local Authorities, Housing Associations and other Social Landlords will have to look into ways of ensuring that their rent recovery system is upgraded and more effective in line with these changes.

SIGNIFICANCE OF RENT COLLECTION

Social Landlords maximise their rent collection due to the following reasons:

1. Backbone for survival.

2. To support service delivery.

3. To maintain essential services such as repairs and maintenance.

4. To cover staff salaries.

5. To satisfy the Housing and Communities Agency.

6. To consolidate for void loss.

7. To pay for loan.

8. Political weapon.

METHODS OF RENT COLLECTION

Various methods of rent collection are necessary in order to expand the payment options available to tenants. They include:

1. Rent card

2. Computerised plastic cards

3. Bank giro

4. Standing order

5. Postal order

6. Post office giro

7. Cashier in the office

8. Direct debit

9. Online payment

10. Deduction from Earnings

11. Rent Collector (Door to Door, Traditional method)

12. Social security direct deductions

13. Invoicing of Local Authorities

14. Other various new methods

CAUSES OF RENT ARREARS

1. Change of circumstances

2. Relationship breakdown

3. Job Loss / Irregular Income

4. Change of employment

5. Ill health

6. Personal development/Education

7. Family growth

8. Unacknowledged rent change

9. Housing Benefit delays

10. Government policies

11. Long term welfare entanglement

12. Adaptation to independency

13. Poverty

14. Excessive debt and prioritising of needs

15. Easy access to credit

16. Management inefficiency

17. Late payment

18. Rent strike

19. Poor financial management

ROLE OF A RENT OFFICER

1. To ensure that maximum rent is collected from their clients.

2. To ensure that the financial information of tenants are obtained before signing the Tenancy Agreement.

3. To reduce the level of rent arrears for its Organisation by effective monitoring and review.

4. To ensure that residents receiving benefits, claim all the benefits they are entitled to.

5. To highlight the Rent Payment Clause in the tenancy agreement and establish a sense of responsibility for tenants regarding their rent payment and benefit take-up at the beginning of the tenancy.

6. To assist with Housing Benefit claim forms.

7. To provide all methods of rent payment options.

8. To encourage the setting up of standing orders or direct debit.

9. To minimise evictions and bad debts for the Organisation.

10. To liaise with Housing Benefit, Social Services and other external agencies with regards to rent payment.

11. To identify and provide support to the vulnerable tenants with regard to their rent payment. Where applicable to refer the tenant to the external agencies that provide tenancy support, which is based on an agreement that the agencies have with the Housing Provider.

12. To strictly comply with the Organisation arrears policy and not be carried away with emotion.

13. To evaluate staff training on Welfare Benefits and debt management.

RENT ARREARS CONTROL

It is very important that the following are in operation to facilitate an effective Rent Collection and Arrears Control System:

1. Direct contact with tenants:

This is the most important aspect in controlling and preventing rent arrears from increasing. It is very important to make a visit to a tenant as soon as any development of arrears arises. This will give you an opportunity to discuss what the problem is and to discuss the way forward with the tenant. The tenant can be contacted as follows:

- By phone

- In writing

- Home visits to the tenant

- Weekly surgeries in the office

2. Pre-action Protocol

All social landlords and Local authorities must ensure that pre-action protocol for rent arrears is in place for their tenants. This can be carried out by the housing providers or a separate agency. This is to ensure that all means have been exhausted before the Landlord seeks to take legal action against its tenant.

3. A detailed Rent Arrears policy:

Organisations must have specific procedures and policies to address the increasing rent arrears problem. This may result in legal action being taken against the tenant.

4. **Good working relationship with Housing Benefit:**

It is very important that Registered Social Landlords have a Liaison Officer who works with the Housing Benefit Department. They should have a Service Level Agreement and must work together to reduce the rent arrears of the Organisation.

RENT COLLECTION AND ARREARS MONITORING

It is very important that you monitor the progress of your rent collection and arrears to enable you to monitor the progress you have made towards the Organisation's set target. The tools include:

1. Weekly Rent Sheet

2. Arrears Record

3. Computerised system

4. Weekly or Monthly Chart

NEW PROTOCOL FOR RENT ARREARS CASES

"The Pre-action Protocol for Rent Arrears was added to court rules and came into force 2 October 2006. It is directly applicable to all rent arrears-based possession claims issued by social landlords. The aim is to encourage more contact between landlords and tenants before court action is taken. Courts are required to take account of whether the protocol has been followed when deciding on what order to make."[7]

The key features of the protocol are:

1. "Landlords should contact tenants as soon as possible after arrears accrue and discuss causes, benefits available, and options for resolving the situation. Agreed repayment plans must be affordable and take proper account of the tenant's income and expenditure patterns.

2. Landlords must ensure that the tenant understands all information provided.

3. Landlords must assist tenants in claiming Housing Benefit and where applicable arrange for direct payments to be paid to the landlord. Landlords should also assist in resolving any Housing Benefit problems.

4. Landlords must not instigate claims for possession where it can be shown that there is a pending Housing Benefit claim with a reasonable expectation of the tenant being eligible. The tenant must be able to demonstrate that the claim has been submitted. This guidance does not apply to landlords' claims not covered by Housing Benefit payments.

5. Quarterly rent statements must be produced, showing the amount due and payments made during the past 13 weeks.

6. Landlords should advise tenants with rent arrears to consult a debt advice agency, as other debts may also be a problem.

7. Following the service of a Notice of Seeking Possession and before starting court action, the landlord must contact the tenant and discuss the arrears, repayment proposals and progress in claiming Housing Benefit.

8. Where the tenant is complying with a reasonable pattern of arrears repayment, court action should not be progressed.

9. Even in the absence of satisfactory repayment arrangements being adhered to, the landlord must advise the tenant to comply with such arrangements and afford reasonable time to do so before instigating court action.

10. If court action is started, the landlord must give details of the date and time of the hearing to the tenant, as well as a warning on the consequences of losing their home. A record must be kept of such notifications.

11. The landlord must provide the tenant with updated rent statements and disclose knowledge of the tenant's Housing Benefit position at least ten days before the date of the court hearing.

12. If after the issue of court action, the tenant agrees to comply with a repayment agreement, then the court action should be postponed.

13. Where subsequently an agreement falls through and the landlord decides to reinstate the court action, then the tenant must be advised of this and given time to comply with the failed agreement.

14. A court can take into consideration whether or not a landlord has complied with the protocol and where it considers that there has been unreasonable failure to do so; it can dismiss the claim."[8]

Some Local Authorities and Housing providers work with other external agencies to provide the Pre-action protocol for rent arrears. Once the tenant is two weeks in arrears, the Housing Officer will refer the case to the agency to work closely with the tenant to avoid legal action being taken against the tenant.

The agency liaises closely with the Income Team or Housing Officer regarding the detail work and support that has been provided to the tenant to ensure that they pay their rent. Where there is evidence that the pre-court protocol has been exhausted and the tenant has failed to work with the agency, a decision will be made to proceed to legal action as required.

PROCEDURE FOR TAKING LEGAL ACTION

Legal Action may be necessary as a last resort when all arrears procedures have been channelled but yield no result. Notice of Seeking Possession must only be served when all steps have been taken. You may have to consider the type of tenancy or Licence you issued. Below are the list of different tenancies issued by Housing Association and Local Authorities:

1. Secured Tenancy

2. Assured Tenancy

3. Assured Short-hold Tenancy

4. Sub-Tenancy Agreement

5. License

All the above tenancies have their legal implications as to what type of Notice to serve and period of Notice that is required.

See Table Below for Type of Tenancy, Landlords and Notice required

TENANCY	LANDLORD	TYPE OF NOTICE	LIFESPAN	NOTICE PERIOD
Secured	Local Authority	NOSP	1 Year	1 month
Assured	Housing Association	NOSP	1 Year	1 month
Assured Shorthold	Housing Associations Private Landlord	NOSP	--	2 months
Licence	Mostly Housing Associations	Notice to Quit	End of the notice period	It varies usually 14 days
Sub-Tenancy	Local Authorities	Notice to Quit	End of the notice period	1 month

RENT MONITORING PROCESS

The Rent Arrears Policy should be implemented once the rent account goes into two weeks in arrears. The stages are:

1. Week two - A telephone call to the tenant as a reminder and the start of the Pre-action protocol for rent arrears.

2. Week Three - A letter to the tenant advising them about the need to pay their rent.

3. Week Four - Another letter and a phone call to the tenant. Set an arrears agreement with the tenant and assist tenant where there are Housing Benefit queries.

4. Week Five - Home visit is required to find out the reason for the delay in the payment of their rent.

5. Week Six - Notice of Seeking Possession is served, this can vary due to the pre-action protocol.

6. Week 7 - Another home visit should be carried out. If tenant is still not co-operating and no payment has been made, continue with the next stage of the policy. However, if the tenant is on Housing Benefit, all matters relating to the benefit must be addressed and resolved (with proper documentation of the actions taken) before legal action can be considered.

7. Week 8 - Apply for court action, obtain authorisation and prepare court papers. Note that court application most be four weeks after the NOSP has been served and the tenant must be kept informed of your intention to proceed to legal action.

8. Week 9 - Contact the tenant to bring the rising arrears to their attention.

9. Week 10 - week 13 Continue to contact the tenant via phone and in writing, until the arrears are cleared or you receive a court hearing date.

10. Week 14 - Court action.

MAKING AN APPLICATION FOR LEGAL PROCEDURE

1. Use a checklist to ensure that all relevant matters have been considered.

2. Ensure that there is no disrepair issue within the property. A potential disrepair claim will certainly result in a contra indicator to issue possession proceedings against the Organisation.

3. Ensure you have authority to issue proceedings.

4. Ensure that all of the Organisation's internal procedures have been adhered to before the issue of proceedings.

5. Ensure that you have complied with the Homes and Communities Agency's guidance.

6. Ensure that the tenant is in breach of the terms of any agreement reached.

7. The Housing Officer must make sure there is a tenancy agreement kept on a file to validate your right of applying for possession. Unavailability of a tenancy agreement invalidates any application. Any legal action cannot stand without the tenancy agreement. It is therefore vital that a copy of the tenancy agreement is kept on file.

8. To avoid delay in possession action, the application form must be properly completed without any error as this is a legal issue with a tenant who is at risk of losing their home. The Court is always careful to ensure that no error has been made. Any single mistake will result in the whole application being sent back to the Organisation for amendment.

DOCUMENTS FOR COURT APPLICATION

The following are the documents required for court application:

1. The Particulars of claim form - Form N119

2. N5 form - Possession Claim form with a statement of Truth

3. Notice of Seeking Possession or Notice to Quit

4. A copy of a signed and dated Tenancy Agreement

5. Copy of the rent statement at the time of application

6. Court Fee

DOCUMENT FOR COURT HEARING

The following are the documents you need to bring when attending the court hearing:

1. Original Tenancy Agreement

2. Notice of Seeking Possession or Notice to Quit

3. Rent Statement indicating current balance

4. Tenants file Containing Arrears Recovery letters and Arrears agreement

5. Affidavit if NOSP is not served by attending member of staff

6. Management Agreement (If managing property on behalf of another landlord)

GROUNDS FOR POSSESSION

The following are the various types of Grounds which the court uses to end a tenancy:

1. Ground 1

2. Ground 8

3. Ground 10

4. Ground 11

1. GROUND 1

This is used for Secured Tenancy. For secure tenants there is only one option which is Ground 1 Schedule 2 of the Housing Act 1985 which states thus:

"Rent lawfully due from the tenant has not been paid or an obligation of the tenancy has been broken or not performed".[9]

2. GROUND 8

This ground is used on Assured Tenancies only. It is a mandatory ground for possession if at the serving of the notice and at the date of the court hearing; the tenant's rent account is sufficiently in arrears. The relevant amount of arrears depends on the rental period:

- ❖ Eight weeks in arrears (weekly and fortnightly tenancies)

- ❖ Two months in arrears (rent payable monthly)

The Housing Act 1998 provides Ground 8. Please note that the landlord only needs to prove the facts of the case to the court but does not need to demonstrate that it is reasonable to grant possession. For mandatory Ground 8, the court can only give an outright possession. However, this cannot be used on vulnerable clients.

3. GROUND 10

This is used on Assured Tenancy and is a discretionary ground for possession when the rent is in arrears on the date when the notice of seeking possession is served and on the date when legal proceedings for possession begins. However, if the tenant pays up in full before the date of a fixed hearing, the case cannot go ahead and that particular Notice cannot be used again. This Ground is covered by the Housing Act 1988.

In this Ground the landlord must satisfy the court that it is reasonable to grant a possession order. The court may suspend the order or postpone the date of possession in these cases.

4. GROUND 11

This is also used on Assured Tenancies. Persistent failure to pay the rent on time is a discretionary ground for possession, regardless of whether the tenant is in arrears on the dates when the notice is served. This

Ground is unlikely to succeed unless Ground 10 is also applied and it is provided by the Housing Act 1988.

AT THE COURT

THE PLAYERS

The major players are:

1. Ushers
2. Judges/Recorders
3. District Judges
4. The tenant
5. Solicitors/ Barristers

IMPORTANT POINTS TO NOTE

1. Possession proceedings were until 26 April 1999 normally dealt with in the County Courts in open court. That is anyone was entitled to sit in Court and hear the proceedings. Now these cases are mostly heard privately in County Courts.

2. Possession proceedings can be dealt with either by a Circuit Judge, a Recorder, or by a District Judge.

3. A circuit Judge or a Recorder is addressed as "your Honour".

4. A District Judge is addressed as "Sir" or "Madam".

5. As a matter of courtesy, where the tenant attends, he or she should always be referred to with the appropriate prefix, Mr, Mrs, or Ms.

6. Where the tenant is represented by a solicitor, barrister or duty adviser, you should endeavour to find out their surname and address them with the usual prefix Mr, Mrs or Ms.

ISSUES AND APPLICATIONS

1. LEAVE TO AMEND

This is mainly to do with defective notices. Where inaccurate particulars are given, the Court may (depending upon the degree of inaccuracy) permit that the matter proceeds or allows amendment of the Notice or the error.

2. REASONABLENESS

This is a pre-condition to granting a Possession Order on any of the discretionary grounds. The Court must be satisfied not only that the Ground itself is proved but that it is reasonable to make an Order for Possession.

In considering this issue, the Court is entitled to take into account all relevant circumstances as they exist at the date of the hearing.

The following are the types of matters which the Court will normally regard as relevant factors to be considered:

- The length of the tenancy.

- The past rent record.

- Establish if the failure to pay rent is persistent.

- The measures taken by the landlord before coming to Court.

- The current circumstances of the tenant and his/her household.

- Whether there have been previous agreements to clear the arrears.

- The tenant's Housing Benefit situation.

3. ADJOURNMENTS

Court hearings can be adjourned to a fixed date, or adjourned generally with or without terms. The Court has inherent power to adjourn proceedings.

The Court also has statutory power to adjourn in the Housing Acts 1985 and 1988, but this statutory power in Section 9 of the 1988 Housing Act does not apply where the mandatory Ground 8 is being used by the landlord.

Where there is outstanding Housing Benefit queries the County Court will exercise their power to adjourn, to enable the queries to be addressed.

The Court requires the hearing to be restored to Court within 6-12 months; failure to do this will result in the case being struck out.

COURT ORDERS

1. Suspended Possession Order

This is the normal order given in residential possession proceedings. This however has been reviewed and is no longer in use in most County Courts since July 2006.

The form N28 must be used. It is important that the SPO be worded correctly to ascertain the precise date when the tenancy began.

Form N28 makes it clear that the landlord's ability to enforce the order ceases once the judgment debt has been cleared.

2. Outright Possession Order

The form N26 is used and it requires that the whole debt be paid off at once. Failure to do this results in the claimant taking possession of the property. This Order provides that the landlord's ability to enforce the order ceases once the Judgment debt has been cleared.

3. Postponed Possession Orders

This was introduced in 2006 to replace Suspended Possession Orders. "The House of Lords judgment introduced the concept of a "tolerated trespasser", being a former tenant who occupied the premises after the expiry of an outright order for Possession and who was subject to an agreement that upon his or her complying with an agreement to a pay a sum equivalent to the rent and a regular sum in reduction of the arrears, the landlord would forebear from executing the Possession Order."[10]

In this case, the Court of Appeal held that the tenancy shall continue until there is a breach of the terms of the Order. Therefore the landlord is free to treat the tenant as a trespasser and to ask the Court to issue a Warrant of Possession.

A Postponed Order means that the terms will be granted but the tenancy will not end (as a tolerated trespasser) if the agreement is breached.

1. Postponed Possessions with an end date is mainly used for Assured Tenancies.

2. Postponed Possessions with no end date are used for Secured Tenancies.

PRESENTING YOUR EVIDENCE

1. Ensure you arrive early.

2. Be smartly dressed and relaxed.

3. Register your name and the Organisation you are representing, as well as the case or cases with the usher.

4. If you see the tenant in court, speak to them and try and agree on the current level of the arrears and a repayment agreement. If you are taking an order against the tenant, advise them to see the Duty Solicitor.

5. Ensure that all your papers are in order and can be easily produced to the judge.

6. If you are requesting for an order, you will normally be sworn in or asked to make an affirmation.

7. You will need to give the following preliminary particulars either of your own accord, or at the request of the Judge:

    - Your full name
    - Your business address
    - Your occupation

8. Also confirm the property you will be addressing, the tenant involved and the tenancy type.

9. Produce the notice served and the Tenancy Agreement.

10. Confirm whether the notice was served by you, whether there is a certificate or affidavit/affirmation of service or whether you recognize the signature of the person who served the notice.

11. Produce an up to date copy of the tenant's rent statement. Also confirm what effort has been made to contact the tenant during the period when they were in arrears.

    This should include:

    - The number of occasions you have written to them.

- The number of times you have had contact with the client.

- Give details of recent contact.

- Give details of proposals made and broken, or any failure on the part of the tenant to respond.

12. Explain the terms of the order that you are seeking. You must ensure that the tenant can reasonably manage; on the basis of information given to you about the tenant's income, or information which you have received from other sources.

13. Ask the Judge to make the following orders:

- An order for Possession suspended on terms.

- Judgment for the rent arrears.

- An order for costs (normally limited to the Court issue fee of £150.00).

14. If at any stage you are in difficulties or are met with a novel point raised by the tenant's solicitor which is likely to sink your claim, always remember that you can request for an adjournment from the Judge in order to enable you seek legal advice.

ENFORCEMENT

Where the tenant has breached the terms of a Suspended Possession Order the order can be enforced. This is by the issue of a Bailiff Warrant to evict the tenant. The ability to issue a Warrant is subject to a limitation period of six years from the date of the order.

DOCUMENTS FOR A BAILIFF WARRANT TO EVICT

1. Request for the Warrant of Possession of Land form.

2. A supporting Witness Statement.

3. Court issue fee irrespective of the amount of the debt.

OTHER IMPORTANT INFORMATION

1. Note that any time up until the date on which the Warrant is executed the tenant has a right to ask the Court to stay or suspend the Warrant. It is not unusual for such applications to be made at the last moment and listed at very short notice.

2. Provided some explanation is offered for non-payment most courts and most Judges will be inclined to give most tenants another chance.

3. However, where there is no application made to suspend a Warrant of Possession, the eviction will be executed by the Bailiff on the required date. The tenant then becomes a former tenant.

FORMER TENANT RENT ARREARS

Former tenant rent arrears can be defined as rent arrears due to the landlord not collecting the rent during the period of the former tenant.

Arrears can be classified in this category as a result of abandonment, in-house transfer or management transfer, move-on, evictions etc. Effort should be made to recover monies owed by ex-tenants, to minimize the organisation losses from bad debts.

FACTORS TO CONSIDER WHEN CHASING FORMER TENANT ARREARS

It is very important to consider the level of arrears to determine if it is cost effective to pursue. The factors to be considered are:

1. Level of arrears owed

2. Circumstances of former tenants

3. Arrears history

4. Employment status

5. Likelihood of recovering

As almost 95% of former tenant rent arrears are due to abandonment, it is very likely that a lot of effort will be required to chase and locate the forwarding address of such tenants.

Abandonment can be defined as a situation whereby a tenant leaves the property without leaving a forwarding address and fails to notify the landlord of their intention to move out of the property.

HOW TO OBTAIN A FORWARDING ADDRESS

1. Neighbours or Friends

2. Colleges/Universities

3. Employers

4. Gas Board

5. Electricity Board

6. Post Office

7. Bank

8. Benefit agency

9. Local Authorities Housing Waiting List

Please note that it may be difficult and frustrating to obtain this information from the above, even when the tenants have business with them. Under the Code of Confidential Act, businesses, especially financial institutions, may be legally prevented from revealing their clients, personal information to a third party.

However, there is a greater chance of being successful with a similar public body such as the Local Authorities and other Government Departments, on the grounds that you can substantially prove your case. For example, state the purpose of your enquiry in your correspondence, which should be written on letter headed paper and include your status.

When requesting such information it is very important to be patient as it may take a minimum of three months for the required information to come to light.

FORMER TENANT WITH FORWARDING ADDRESS

A standard policy and procedure for dealing with Former Tenants Arrears should be in place. This should include the following:

1. Contact the former tenant in writing reminding them of outstanding arrears. This should also include details of when the arrears were accrued, name of staff to contact to arrange how and when arrears can be paid.

2. Failure to respond: send a reminder letter about arrears and stress the need to contact the organisation within the next seven days. Emphasize the implications of not paying rent arrears; such as legal action and the consequence of it on their credit record.

3. If no response to the letters is received, a home visit should be carried out - depending on distance.

4. If the former tenant is still not complying with your request then Legal action to recover the arrears via money judgment or attachment to earning can commence. Please note that this can only be applied to a working former tenant and not a claimant. Legal action may not be necessary where the level of arrears owed is minimal, or where the former tenant is a claimant.

JUDGEMENT ENFORCEMENT

Formal application to Local County Court is required and this can only apply to working ex-tenants. There are two methods of enforcement:

1. Attachment of Earnings: This is whereby the Court orders the former tenant's employer to make certain fixed deductions from their earnings.

2. Garnishee Order: This is whereby the Court applies to the former tenant's bank requesting money in the account to be used to set off the arrears.

FORMER TENANT ARREARS DUE TO HOUSING BENEFIT

Where arrears are due to Housing Benefit, because the former tenant did not provide the requested information at the time of his tenancy, the following needs to be carried out:

1. Information can be obtained from the ex-tenants and necessary letters signed by them.

2. Documents can be forwarded to Housing Benefit with a strong supported letter such as vulnerability of the tenant (now a former tenant). The purpose is to convince Housing Benefit of the reason why the tenant's Housing Benefit should be backdated.

3. Put in a request for the Housing Benefit to be backdated. Housing Benefit will backdate a claim over a period of one year. However, this is in exceptional circumstances and with supporting evidence.

4. Former tenants should be alerted that their physical presence might be required by Housing Benefit, in some circumstances before their claim can be backdated. Tenants should make themselves available if any such demand is requested by Housing Benefit.

Please note that when dealing with former tenant from this category it is very important to be as friendly as you can, in order to derive their ultimate co-operation.

It is always important to be highly diplomatic and supportive, in order to enhance the tenant's participation in the recovery of their arrears. We must bear in mind that non-cooperation may result in eligible rent arrears never being collected.

Chapter Seven

ANTI SOCIAL BEHAVIOUR

WHAT CONSTITUTES ANTI-SOCIAL BEHAVIOUR?

Anti social behaviour is defined as:

"Behaviour that causes or is likely to cause harassment, alarm or distress to a person".

The term is sometimes used interchangeably with the term 'nuisance'. Nuisance is any behaviour that unreasonably interferes with a person's use and enjoyment of their property, while anti-social behaviour is normally associated with serious and or sub-criminal behaviour.

Examples of what could be regarded as anti-social behaviour and/or a nuisance could include the following:

1. Using or threatening violence

2. Playing loud music

3. Banging and slamming doors

4. Abusive language

5. Dog barking and fouling

6. Street or residential drug dealing

7. Graffiti

8. Offensive drunkenness

9. Criminal activities

10. Racial harassment

11. Noise and nuisance behaviour

12. Vandalism

13. Domestic Violence

14. Damage to property

15. Neighbour disputes

Social Landlords and Local Authority's approach in dealing with anti-social behaviour is to support the right of tenants to live in peace and quietness in their own homes, as long as they do not interfere in the peace and quietness of others. They work with tenants and other agencies to take action to stop anti-social behaviour by responding to such complaints quickly and in an efficient, sensitive and consistent manner. Their role is to offer support to the victim and take action against those responsible for such actions.

Landlords will need to investigate all complaints and take a complainant-centered approach. They are to encourage tenants to attempt to resolve problems themselves in the first instance, supporting them with information, advice and the offer of mediation.

WHO DEALS WITH ASB CASES?

Anti-social behaviour cases need a multi-agency approach. These include:

1. Housing Officers
2. Estate Services Officers
3. Housing Managers
4. Caretakers
5. Schools
6. Police Officers
7. Environmental Health
8. Play and Youth Education
9. Social Landlords
10. Local Authority
11. Other Support Agencies

CHOOSING THE RIGHT ACTION

Legal vs. Non-legal action

1. Legal action is not always effective and it can take a long time.
2. Informal action can be very quick and 'nip the problem in the bud', which avoids the escalation of the problem.

3. The punishment of the perpetrators should not be the aim of landlords, unlike the complainants. Their aim should be to stop the nuisance.

4. Legal action is not always appropriate because the response has to 'be proportionate to the wrong doing'.

5. Start off with an informal approach by trying to reach an agreement to a change in behaviour.

6. The use of informal agreements, that are not legally binding, should be used. These can be powerful supporting evidence in court.

7. It is very important to note that doing nothing is not an option. It will only attract complaints against the Organisation from solicitors, residents, Councillors and the Ombudsman.

OPPORTUNITIES TO EDUCATE YOUR TENANTS ON ASB DURING SIGN UPS

First impressions is a very important tool in highlighting your Organisation's stand with respect to Anti-Social Behaviour.

What are you and your Organisation projecting?

1. Image

2. Professionalism

3. Project safety and commitment to tenants through boundaries

4. The word will spread (What are people saying about the Organisation?)

5. Rubbish

6. Dumped vehicles

7. Broken windows syndrome

8. Noise

9. Strong odours

10. Front gardens

THE MAIN PROCESS

The main step is to explain the Tenancy Agreement to your client and this involves the following:

1. Explaining that the tenancy agreement is a legal document that constitutes a legal agreement.

2. Highlighting the need for accountability and responsibility is therefore vital.

3. Explaining that a breach of agreement could lead to court action and legal fees being incurred.

4. Consider the use of a signed 'checklist' to show that the information received is understood, including the possible consequences if the agreement is breached.

5. Encourage all members of the household to be present including the children.

THE CHOICE OF LOCATION FOR THE SIGN UP

This can either be in the main office, or on the estate where your client will be living. The following points need to be taken into consideration:

1. There will be pros and cons in any location.

2. Consider the role of the site based staff at the sign up.

3. Introduce tenants to the tenant participation scheme and the tenant representative for that estate.

4. Seek permission to pass their details to the Neighbourhood Watch coordinator for an introductory visit where available.

5. Give examples of what constitutes a breach of tenancy and let them know your Organisation's stand on such breaches.

6. Follow up visits should be carried out about 4 to 6 weeks after the sign up to ensure that the tenant has settled down and all outstanding issues are addressed.

It is crucial that the prospective tenant understands the concept of ownership and accountability. This is intervention by the early reinforcement of responsibilities and consequences and it serves as a preventive measure.

TOOL FOR EARLY INTERVENTIONS

This includes the following:

1. Use of warnings

2. Acceptable Behaviour Contract or Agreement

3. Partnership Working

4. Mediation

5. Anti-Social Behaviour Orders

GUIDELINES IN DEALING WITH ASB ISSUES

1. When a complaint is received, ascertain whether it is a minor or major problem.

2. Always arrange an appointment to see the complainant in person, to obtain full details of the complaint and agree an action plan.

3. Carry out further investigation where appropriate before contacting the perpetrator.

4. Arrange to address the allegation with the perpetrator.

5. Choose how to respond with the aim of addressing the issue immediately.

6. The use of verbal and written warnings can be implemented in the early stages. However, if there is no improvement further action can be implemented.

7. Where appropriate, you can involve other agencies and start to create a case conference. This may also involve the use of mediation.

ACCEPTABLE BEHAVIOUR CONTRACTS

Acceptable Behaviour Contracts (ABC) is a way in which Crime and Disorder Partnerships can tackle anti-social behaviour, particularly among teenagers as well as adults. The contracts may serve as a useful alternative to tackle Anti-Social Behaviours where the latter are not considered justified.

Other additional facts about the contract are:

1. ABCs can be put into effect within days and at little cost.

2. Where an ABC is breached by an individual who constitutes to act in a manner which causes harassment, that fact can be used as evidence in support of an Anti-Social Behaviour Order application.

3. An Acceptable Behaviour Contract is a written agreement by a young person or adult with a partner agency and the police to not carry on certain identified acts, which could be construed as anti-social behaviour.

4. It has been designed for 10 to 18 year olds, although it is flexible and can be used occasionally, where appropriate, for 18 year olds if they live at home in council, rented or privately owned property with their parents.

5. It can also be used for adults as a soft approach in tackling the anti-social behaviour.

ACCEPTABLE BEHAVIOUR CONTRACTS UNDER 10

1. In cases where a child is under 10, the parents could be asked to sign a parental responsibility contract. This would be the same as an ABC except that the parents take full responsibility for their child's behaviour.

2. An ABC is not legally binding but it could be cited in proceedings such as for Anti-Social Behaviour Order.

3. An ABC should normally be effective for up to six months, although it can be renewed.

4. Arrangements should be made by the partner agency and the police to monitor the ABC's effectiveness and to keep the terms under review.

5. An agency official and police officer should be present, as well as the young person's parent or guardian and any other appropriate adult, such as a social worker, concerned for the young person's welfare, when signing the agreement.

6. If the young person fails to attend despite a letter of invitation sent to him or her and to the parent or guardian, the non-appearance should be documented and used at future proceedings.

7. If the young person attends but the parent refuses to, then the contract signing may still go ahead, provided an appropriate adult is present.

8. The original contract is kept by the partner agency; a copy is kept by the police and a copy is given to the parent/ guardian of the youth concerned.

9. If the ABC is breached, and the breach is serious, the matter should be referred to the partnership's problem solving group for a decision as to the most effective course of action, including an ASBO.

10. If the breach is not serious, the parents and young person should either be interviewed or sent a letter reiterating the conditions of the contract.

Adelola Dairo

ACCEPTABLE BEHAVIOUR CONTRACT

THIS CONTRACT is made on   DATE

BETWEEN   PARTNER AGENCY

AND   SUBJECT NAME, ADDRESS & D.O.B.

AGREES the following in respect of future conduct—

I will or will not (specify where)
I will or will not . . . .
I will or will not (specify where)
I will or will not

FURTHER, NAME OF SUBJECT enters into a commitment with PARTNER AGENCY not to act in a manner which causes or is likely to cause harassment, alarm or distress to one or more persons not in the same household.

FURTHER, NAME OF SUBJECT does anything which he/she has agreed not to do under this contract which ABOVE PARTNERS considers to amount to Anti-Social Behaviour, this may result in an application to the Magistrate Court for an Anti-Social Behaviour Order to prohibit NAME OF SUBJECT from acting in a manner which causes or is likely to cause harassment, alarm, or distress to one or more persons not in the same household.

FURTHER, NAME OF SUBJECT acknowledges that where an Anti-Social Behaviour Order is made by the Court and breached he/she will be liable for conviction and terms of imprisonment not exceeding five years, or a fine, or both.

DECLARATION

I confirm that I understand the meaning of this contract and that the consequences of breach of the contract have been explained to me.

Housing Management Simplified

Signed _____   NAME OF SUBJECT
Date _____

Signed _____   Parent
Date _____

WITNESSED

Signed _____   Partner Agency Official
Date _____

Signed _____   Police Officer
Date _____

PARENTAL CONTROL AGREEMENT

THIS CONTRACT is made on   DATE

BETWEEN   PARTNER AGENCY

AND   PARENT NAME & ADDRESS

AGREES the following in respect of future conduct of Subject's Name

I will or l will not . . . . (Specify)
I will or l will not . . . .
I will or l will not . . . . (Specify)
I will or l will not . . . .

FURTHER, NAME OF PARENT enters into a commitment with PARTNER AGENCY not to allow SUBJECT'S NAME act in a manner which causes, or is likely to cause harassment, alarm or distress to one or more persons not in the same household.

FURTHER, NAME OF PARENT must not allow SUBJECT'S NAME to do anything which he/she has agreed not to do under this contract which ABOVE PARTNERS considers to amount to Anti-Social Behaviour. This may result in an application to the Magistrate Court for an Anti-Social Behaviour Order to prohibit NAME OF PARENT to allow SUBJECT'S NAME from acting in a manner which causes or is likely to cause harassment, alarm, or distress to one or more persons not in the same household.

DECLARATION

I confirm that l understand the meaning of this contract and that the consequences of breach of the contract have been explained to me.

Signed _____   NAME OF PARENT

Date _____

WITNESSED

Signed _____   Partner Agency Official

Date _____

Signed _____   Police Officer

Date _____

MEDIATION

WHAT IS MEDIATION?

"Mediation is a process whereby a neutral third party enables two or more parties in dispute to seek a mutually acceptable resolution to their difficulties without resource to formal or legal procedures."[11]

Mediation is about:

1. Exploring emotions
2. Identifying key issues
3. Negotiation
4. Creating options
5. Breaking the "cycle of dispute"
6. Focusing on the future

It is not about:

1. Apportioning blame
2. Passing judgments
3. Gathering evidence
4. Giving advice

Mediation is appropriate when both parties:

1. Voluntarily choose it
2. Are willing to be reasonable

3. Are willing for the other side to be contacted

4. Are able to communicate

It is not appropriate when:

1. One party is intent on punishing the other.

2. An imbalance of power exists which impedes honest exchange.

3. Either party fears or is placed at risk of violence, racial abuse or sexual harassment.

MEDIATION MODELS

Direct mediation-round table mediation

1. Mediators will visit each party.

2. They will explore the emotions and the issues that are central to the dispute.

3. If the parties are willing to meet and the mediators think it is appropriate, they will arrange to meet on neutral grounds to discuss their dispute.

4. A "round table" mediation session follows a very specific format that includes:

    - Periods of uninterrupted time for each party to express their feelings without fear of being challenged.

Indirect mediation

1. This is where parties are unwilling to meet.

2. Mediators will visit each party in turn.

3. They will seek to identify issues that are central to the dispute and explore the emotions that surround them.

4. Mediators will, with permission of both parties, engage by acting as an intermediary, conveying messages between each of the parties.

5. This may continue for a number of weeks until both parties feel able to enter into some form of agreement.

6. Agreements can be verbal or written and are very specific. A written agreement will be constructed using the parties' own words. Verbal agreements can have as much force as written agreements.

SUPPORT TO ONE PARTY

This is where only one of the parties may wish to proceed with the process of mediation.

In these circumstances, some mediation services will assist this party by helping them to find constructive ways of handling their responses in the dispute.

ANTI-SOCIAL BEHAVIOUR ORDERS (ASBOs)

The anti-social behaviour order is not a tool to settle private disputes between two or more neighbouring families (for example, over boundary lines). This is a tool to combat anti-social behaviour by one or more people in a neighbourhood, which makes life a misery for others.

Note the following:

1. Originally only Local Authorities and the police could apply for anti-social behaviour orders, but the Police Reform Act 2002 extended the powers to Housing Associations.

2. Housing Associations can apply for an ASBO from a magistrate court when a person (over the age of ten) has been behaving in an anti-social manner, and it is necessary to protect others from further anti-social behaviour by that person.

3. An ASBO remains in force for at least two years and a breach is a criminal offence, which can attract stiff penalties of up to five years' imprisonment.

4. ASBOs are an important addition to the range of responses available to tackle racist perpetrators.

5. ASBOs can be sought against an individual whose behaviour has caused harassment, alarm or distress to anyone outside their own household. This means that ASBOs can be used against a range of racist perpetrators including youths, older children and adults.

6. The flexibility of the Order means that restrictions can be tailored to individual cases. For example, an ASBO could be used to prevent a youth responsible for racial harassment from entering specific parts of a housing estate.

7. There is no requirement to demonstrate that every other remedy has been exhausted before applying for an ASBO. The key is that an ASBO should be used where it is the most appropriate remedy.

8. Subsequent action will depend on what legal remedies are available. However, the principle behind application of the policy remains to ensure that courses of action are agreed with the complainant, that they are kept regularly informed with what is happening, and that cases are closed in a controlled manner.

9. The approach to take when dealing with anti-social behaviour is to work with both parties to resolve their issues. Sometimes situations are complicated and may have escalated on both sides; what the landlord must aim to do is to work with both sides to reach a position where both feel that a satisfactory outcome has been achieved. The basis for this is the action plan.

10. If one party does not want to agree an action plan then this should be recorded on the database.

THE INJUNCTION TO PREVENT NUISANCE AND ANNOYANCE

The Injunction to Prevent Nuisance and Annoyance 'IPNA' is the new name for the Crime Prevention Injunction,[12] which is due to replace the housing-specific Anti-social Behaviour Injunction (ASBI), Anti-Social Behaviour Order (ASBO) on application, intervention orders and individual support orders.

It will cover ages 10 and above (the ASBI and ASBO were aimed at over 18 year olds). The IPNA can be used against any individual, no matter whether they are in social housing or private residents.

As far as the details of the IPNA are concerned, the Home Office has listened to the concerns of housing associations and have tried to replicate the effective and speedy ASBI as far as possible.

The IPNA retains the lower test - nuisance and annoyance - and the lower proof 'balance of probabilities' that already exist for the ASB. It includes provisions for interim, without notice, applications which have proved so successful in the Social Housing world.

The IPNA can be applied for, and breaches dealt with, in the County Courts, which currently handle applications for ASBIs/ASBOs.

Like the ASBI a power of arrest can be attached to prohibitions where there is a risk of significant harm to victims and an exclusion order can be submitted to run along side. The granting of IPNA is to give victims and communities more power to define and respond to anti-social behaviour. It also imposes positive requirements on perpetrators to address the causes of their behaviour.

OTHER PREVENTATIVE ACTION

In order to minimize the risk of anti-social behaviour, other measures that can be taken include:

1. Undertaking a risk assessment when prospective tenants are referred by the local authority, or when tenants transfer into another property.

2. Going carefully through tenant's rights and obligations at sign-up.

3. Publicizing the action we will take if anti-social behaviour occurs.

SUPPORT

In some situations there may be a need for support to be offered to the victim. It may be appropriate, for example, to approach other local agencies to provide this support, depending on what is needed. One option is to refer either the complainant or the person complained about for floating support.

GATHERING EVIDENCE

It is very important to investigate the initial complaint and capitalise on the first interview.

The following six main questions need to be asked:

1. What is the problem?

2. Why is it happening?

3. When; is there a pattern?

4. Where?

5. To whom?

6. What are the effects?

Diaries should be issued out to the complainant to monitor the occurrence of the incident.

LEGAL REMEDIES

CIVIL EVIDENCE ACT 1995

The use of witnesses is vital when presenting a case in a court of Law. This could be in person or hearsay witnesses who can help strengthen your case.

1. The Civil Evidence Act 1985 permits the use of hearsay evidence at trial possession claims and other civil matters is permitted.

2. Proper notice has to be given to the defendant.

3. The defendant can call for the witness to attend court for cross-examination.

4. The above renders anonymous hearsay extremely problematic.

5. There is no history of a defended case succeeding on hearsay evidence alone. It is therefore important to encourage the complainant to be prepared to give witness at court if required.

POSSESSION BASED ON ASB

1. The wording of the ground for possession is the same for Local Authority and Registered Social Landlords (1-14) and both have equal opportunities for action.

2. Clearly documented Housing Management intervention evidence which challenges the perpetrator is key to achieving success.

3. Be willing to move early in the case and achieve a suspended order.

CCTV & OTHER RECORDINGS

1. Video recorded evidence should be dated and time coded. It needs to be clear and verified by someone who can identify the participants and provide a narrative of the action.

2. Audio recordings need to be supported by credible technical evidence which verifies the correct working and accuracy of the recording devices, and confirms the noise source.

3. In respect of both types of evidence, good practice should be followed to preserve the integrity and safe-handling of the recordings, the originals of which should always be kept for production at Court if necessary. It is important to note that they are not always effective tools for court purposes.

INTRODUCTORY TENANCIES

1. An Introductory tenancy is used by the councils as a probationary tenancy and it lasts for 12 months. It gives you the same right as a secure tenancy but you can be easily evicted. If the perpetrator is on such a tenancy, and fails to comply with agreements made to address the behaviour, the tenancy can be terminated at the end of the 12 months as required.

2. The tenancy is ended by Court Order, but the Judge cannot make a Suspended order and has no jurisdiction to suspend or postpone a warrant.

FAMILY LAW ACT 1996

1. This is useful in cases of domestic violence. Where they are joint tenants, a Notice to Quit by one determines the tenancy for both.

2. Occupants have the right to apply to Court to regulate the occupation of the home, and who should hold the tenancy.

3. The tenant has the automatic right to apply for an occupation order.

4. The order can require the applicant to be admitted into the home or exclude the respondent from the home, or a defined area around the home.

5. The Court will consider safety and well-being, housing needs, financial resources, conduct, and the balance of harm.

6. The Court can effectively transfer the tenancy from one occupant to the other and make orders dealing with existing arrears and future rent liability.

INJUNCTIONS

What is an Injunction?

An Injunction order of the court is an order that:

1. Requires someone to commit a specific act (mandatory/positive).

2. Requires someone to refrain from a certain act (prohibitory/negative).

Application for injunctions can be made under the following legal frameworks:

1. Section 153 of the Housing Act 1996

2. Where it has a cause of action in law - for example: Breach of contract (where the tenancy agreement is the contract)

3. Torts (civil wrongs):

   - Nuisance

   - Harassment

   - Trespass

   - Assault

4. The legal process was amended by the Civil Procedure Rules 1998 which came into force on 1 April 1999 as a result of recommendations by Lord Wolf.[13]

5. Applications can be made without giving notice to the defendant (these are referred to as Applications without Notice) and can be heard on the same day in emergencies. In some circumstances courts can even hear cases by telephone.

The following need to be prepared: Claim and Witness statement in support.

6. Applications can be made in anticipation of events which could give rise to a course of action. Such applications are referred to as being *quia timet*. Witness statements replace affidavits, which used to be used. Witness statements must be drawn up in a particular way.

7. Under Section 153 of the Housing Act 1996, registered a Social Landlords can apply for a Power of Arrest to be attached to an injunction for a breach or an anticipated breach of tenancy.

8. When deciding whether such a Power of Arrest should be attached to the injunction, the court must have to decide whether the tenant or any other person - residing in or visiting a property, has used or threatened violence to a person residing, visiting or engaging in a lawful activity. They also have to decide if there is a significant risk of harm to that person if a Power of Arrest is not attached.

Points to bear in mind:

9. Injunctions are difficult to enforce if a perpetrator cannot be linked to a particular tenant.

10. They should not be used against minors.

11. The sanction for imprisonment for contempt of court upon the breach of an injunction may have a persuasive effect in modifying behaviour. (Guidance provided by the Social Landlords Crime and Nuisance Group.)

PROTECTION FROM HARASSMENT ACT 1997

1. The statutory definition of harassment is very wide. "Conduct causing or likely to cause alarm or distress". There is difficulty in deciding the appropriate threshold.

2. Evidence must be provided of a "course of conduct", that is conduct on at least two occasions.

3. Two ways forward: Criminal Prosecution and Civil Injunction (and possible damages).

4. It is important to note that this is a personal remedy and not of the landlord.

5. Breach of any restraining order is an arrestable criminal offence and can constitute grounds for possession.

6. Landlords can assist a tenant to take action against a non-tenant.

USE OF WITNESS STATEMENTS

When taking legal action the use of witness statements is important. A witness statement is a formal document containing your own account of the facts relating to matters arising in a dispute. The purpose of the document is to provide written evidence to support the person's case in court. The statement needs to be accurate and detailed. A witness statement should be prepared by a solicitor to ensure that it achieves the desired effect and result.

Depending on the type of anti-social behaviour case, residents are not always willing to attend court hearings and give statements. However, the Officer dealing with the case on behalf of the landlord can do the witness statements on behalf of the residents. The officer will need to work closely with the solicitor dealing with the case to draft the statement.

Witness statement (model)

IN THE COUNTY COURT

BETWEEN   Case no:
Filed on behalf of:
Deponent:
Statement no:
Date made:
Exhibits: No: to No:

_____ (Claimant)

And _____ (Defendant)

WITNESS STATEMENT OF

I _____ (name and address of Claimant) say as follows

1. I am employed by the Claimant in the capacity of _____ based at the _____ and in this capacity. I am duly authorised to provide this statement in support of the Claimant's action against the defendant.

2. In the course of my employment I am responsible for: (OR altered as above)

3. I make this statement from my own knowledge and from the Claimant's files in this matter.

4. Body of statement:

    a) Differentiate in text between:

       i) Own knowledge
       ii) Information
       iii) Belief

b) State source of matters of:

  i) Information
  ii) Belief

c) Exhibits - must be separate with exhibit sheet. Exhibit ref. must be stated in margin against the relevant paragraph.
d) Exhibits - should be identified in statement: "I refer to the letter dated xxxxx and marked xxxxx.
e) Numbers expressed in figures.
f) All pages must be numbered.

5   I believe that the facts stated in this witness statement are true.

Signed _____

Dated _____

Exhibit front sheet (model)

IN THE COUNTY COURT Case no:
Filed on behalf of:
Deponent:
Statement no:
Date made:
Exhibits: No xx to No xx
This exhibit: xx

BETWEEN

_____ (Claimant)

AND

_____ (Defendant)

This is the exhibit marked xx referred to in the Statement of _____

Signed _____

Dated _____

USEFUL INFORMATION

- It is very important that Social Landlords and other housing providers have set policy and procedures in place to tackle anti-social behaviour. They also have to ensure that the staff assigned to deal with such matters are well trained, and equipped with the necessary tools and support required to deal with the matters effectively.

- A problem solving approach should always be employed by staff members dealing with anti-social behaviour matter; this may sometimes require working outside of the policy. It is important that such actions are confirmed with the staff's line manager before implementation.

- It is important to have some knowledge of the above information when dealing with anti-social behaviour matters. This equips you with other courses of action to take on given cases.

WITNESS INTIMIDATION

Section 39 of the Criminal Justice and Public Order Act 2001 makes it an Offence to intimidate a person whilst knowing or believing that the person is or may be a witness in civil proceedings with the intention of preventing, obstructing or interfering with the course of justice.

1. Intimidation includes threats against any person or against a person's finances or property.

2. The act of intimidation can be in the witnesses' presence or through a third party.

3. Section 40 of the Act makes it an offence to perform an act, which harms and is intended to harm another person, or if it intends to cause another person to fear harm, by threatening to perform an act that would harm the other person. This act must be done in the belief that another person (either the witness or any other person against whom harm is threatened) has been a witness in the proceedings.

4. A conviction under sections 39 or 40 could result in an unlimited fine and/ or a term of imprisonment of up to 5 years.

5. Section 44 of the Act amends the Protection from Harassment Act 1997 to make it an offence for two or more persons to conduct a campaign of harassment.

6. Collective harassment is punishable on summary conviction to the maximum fine or up to six months imprisonment.

Alternatively, on indictment the court can impose up to five years imprisonment and/ or maximum fine.

ENVIRONMENTAL PROTECTION ACT 1990

In the case of excessive noise, noxious smells or fumes, occurring in, or emitting from a premises, that is prejudicial to health or a nuisance, a Local Authority has the power to take action under the EPA 1990. The act places a duty on Local Authorities to take reasonably practical steps to investigate complaints of nuisance made by people in their area.

Part 111 is directed towards abatement of "statutory nuisances" and provides two ways forward:

1. A Local Authority may serve a Notice to Abate the Nuisance (580). Continuance can result in prosecution in the Magistrate's Court and if found guilty, the person responsible may be liable to a fine.

2. A "person Aggrieved can issue a statutory letter and take proceedings in the Magistrates Court against the wrongdoer".[14]

Examples of "Statutory nuisance":

1. Smoke, fumes, dust, gases, accumulations, noisy animals.

2. Which are prejudicial to health or a nuisance that is creating an unreasonable interference with the use or enjoyment of the home?

3. May engage and subsequently breach Human Rights Act Article 8 'Right to respect for private family life'.

THE NOISE ACT 1996

The powers contained in the NA 1996 have to be adopted before it becomes applicable in a Local Authority's area. Under the Act, the authority has a duty to investigate complaints of excessive noise emitted from a dwelling between the hours of 11pm and 7 am.

The authority may serve a 'warning notice' stating an offence is being committed. Failure to comply with the notice could result in person responsible being prosecuted in the Magistrates Court, and be liable if convicted to pay a fine of £1000.

The council has powers to enter premises and seize noise-making equipment. If entry is refused, the Authority can obtain a warrant to enter.

- A "person aggrieved" can issue a statutory letter and take proceedings in the Magistrates Court against the wrongdoer.

Examples of 'Statutory nuisance':

1. Smoke fumes, dust, gases, accumulations, noise, animals.

2. That which are prejudicial to health or a nuisance, that it creates an unreasonable interference with the use or enjoyment of the home.

3. May engage and subsequently breach Human Rights Act Article 8: The 'Right to respect for private and family life'.

NOISE ACT 1996(ii)

The court can, on the complaint of the person aggrieved, order the nuisance to be abated and fine the Defendant. A landlord can be held the "person responsible", even if an occupant creates the nuisance. In addition to the fines, the Court can ward compensations of up to £5,000 to the victim.

THE ROLE OF A HOUSING OFFICER OR ANTI SOCIAL BEHAVIOUR OFFICER

The Anti-Social Behaviour Officer/or Housing Officer plays a vital role in dealing with all matters relating to this anti-social behaviour.

Their role includes the following:

1. Ensuring that all cases of anti-social behaviour reported are logged and responded to in accordance with the company's procedure.

2. Ensuring that contact is made with the complainant either by phone, email, in writing or in person to obtain detailed information on the matter.

3. To be open and honest with the complainant and not make any promises that cannot be achieved.

4. Explain the company's anti-social behaviour policy to the complainant and agree on an action plan with them.

5. Encourage the complainant to approach the alleged perpetrator to bring the matter to their attention, depending on the situation. Examples of such matters are drilling till late at night, making noise etc. This is because the person may not be aware that they were causing a disturbance. If this is ineffective, the officer can proceed to deal with the matter.

6. The Officer should encourage the complainant to start maintaining a log of incidents that occur, as this may be useful should the case require legal action.

7. Contact the alleged perpetrator in writing bringing their attention to the complaint and invite them in for an interview. Interview the resident as required and go through the terms of their tenancy agreement with them.

8. Carry out investigations of the cases reported thoroughly to establish if there is breach in the tenancy agreement. It might involve speaking to other residents in the block to ascertain if there are any anti-social behaviour issues they should be aware of.

9. Seek the appropriate action suitable to the case in order to bring a quick solution to the matter.

10. Apply a multi-agency working approach to resolve some anti-social behaviour. Work very closely with the various external agencies that are also involved in tackling anti-social behaviour. This includes the Noise and Nuisance Team, The Local Police Officers for the area and the Council's Anti-Social Behaviour Team as well as other support agencies connected with the alleged perpetrator.

11. Ensure that a proper recording system is maintained. All letters relating to the case must be well documented and kept. This includes the various actions taken, visits made, agreement breached and warnings served. This is very important, should you need to escalate the case to legal action.

12. Once a case has been dealt with and the matter is resolved, seek to close the case if no further complaint is received after two to three months. Ensure the complainant is notified accordingly.

Chapter Eight

TENANCY MATTERS

ASSIGNMENT

The transferring of tenancy to another person can be carried out in several ways. However, the method of transfer depends on what is available at the time. They depend on the following:

1. The type of tenancy.

2. The reason for the transfer.

3. What the tenancy agreement says.

4. The agreement of the landlord.

One of the main methods of transferring a tenancy from one person to another is by Assignment.

DEFINITION OF ASSIGNMENT

This is the transfer of the tenancy of an existing property from one living person to another. Assignment can be done by the sole tenant or the joint tenants acting together and can be made to any other person or one of the joint tenants. Other points to note include:

1. Assignment is the transfer of the assignor's legal interest in a property to another person, known as the assignee.

2. When a tenant assign's the tenancy, his/her legal interest in the property is passed on to the assignee who takes over that interest and becomes the tenant.

3. Once the assignment has taken place, the landlord and the assignee have a direct landlord/tenant relationship.

4. All the terms of the original tenancy agreement apply to the assignee. The assignee should pay the same rent as the original tenant.

WAYS OF ASSIGNMENT

There are three main ways by which tenants can assign their tenancy. These include:

1. Assignment by Court Order

This is when a court order is granted to transfer the tenancy to a person as a result of a divorce settlement, or under the Children's Act or partners separating. A copy of the Court Order must be attached to the existing tenancy agreement. The transfer takes place immediately, in line with the Order.

2. Assignment by Mutual Exchange

This is when the tenant agrees to exchange their property with another tenant. The tenant makes an application to his/her landlord, who would in turn approve it. Secure and Assured tenants have contractual rights to exchange their property with another Housing Association or Local Authority under their Tenancy Agreement. Note that this is not applicable to Assured Short-hold and Starter tenancies.

3. Assignment to a would-be successor

This is used by landlords mainly by discretion, due to the fact that Secure and Assured tenants do not have a contractual right to assign to a would-be successor under the Standard Tenancy Agreement. It is the process whereby the tenant wants to transfer his/her tenancy to someone entitled to succeed to it. Applications must be made in writing to the landlord, who in turn makes the decision.

HOW TO ASSIGN A TENANCY

1. An Assignment is made by deed. This is a written document which has been signed "as a deed" and witnessed.

2. This deed of assignment needs to be kept by the new tenant in case he/she needs to prove that the assignment has taken place. It is also important that the outgoing tenant has a copy of the deed.

3. The deed must give the full names and addresses of the original tenant and the new tenant.

4. It must also have the details of the landlord and the original date of when the tenancy agreement started, as well as the new date when the assignment began.

5. The signatures of the original tenant and the new tenant must be witnessed by an independent person. The same person can witness all the signatures.

IMPORTANT POINTS TO NOTE

1. Application for assignment has to be made in writing by the original tenant to his/her landlord.

2. The landlord's consent has to be obtained for the assignment to be approved.

3. Most landlords will ensure that the rent account of the tenant applying to assign his/her tenancy is in good order. No possession order must be on the account.

4. The Landlord and Local Authority will only grant one application of assignment on a tenancy agreement.

SUCCESSION

DEFINITION

A Succession is the process whereby on the death of a tenant, the tenancy of the existing property transfers to another resident of the property. There are legal rights of succession, but this differs for both Secure and Assured Tenancy. When dealing with Successions, all gay and lesbian relationships are treated in the same way as heterosexual relationships.

HOW TO QUALIFY FOR A SUCCESSION

The Homes and Communities Agency suggests that Registered Social Landlords should grant the right to succession of a guaranteed offer or a suitable alternative to members of a tenant's family, or same sex partner, providing they meet the following criteria:

1. They have been living with the tenant a year before their death.

2. They have been looking after the tenant.

3. They have accepted responsibility for the tenant's dependents.

4. They would be made homeless if required to leave the accommodation.

For all joint tenancies if one party dies, the other person will be the successor of the tenancy.

IMPORTANT POINTS

1. A succession can only be initiated when a tenant passes away and Social Landlords have set procedures and policies in place to address this.

2. A Successor must be living in the property at the time of the tenant's death.

3. A successor can be the tenant's spouse. A spouse is defined as the husband or wife, or co-habiting partner.

4. A successor can also be another member of the tenant's family who has lived with the tenant 12 months prior to the death of the tenant.

LEGAL BACKGROUND FOR SECURED TENANTS

1. Section 87 of the Housing Act 1985 states that, in England and Wales, when a secure tenant dies the tenancy may be passed to a qualified successor.[15]

2. A qualified successor must have lived in the property as his /her principal home at the time of the death of the tenant.

3. The successor can either be the tenant's spouse or another member of the tenant's family who must have resided in the property 12 months prior to the tenant's death.

4. Where there is more than one qualifying successor, the spouse takes precedence over other relatives.

LEGAL BACKGROUND FOR ASSURED TENANTS

1. This is covered under the Housing Act 1988 section 17, and it limits the right of succession to one.

2. In joint tenancy where one of the tenant dies and neither have been a successor already, the other succeeds.

3. In sole tenancy, the spouse or partner only succeeds if they are living in the property and occupying it as their main home and the sole tenant was not a successor.

4. When there is an under-occupied accommodation by a successor who is not the deceased tenant's spouse, the landlord can seek

possession of the property under Schedule 2, Ground 9. The landlord has to provide suitable replacement accommodation.

5. For Assured Short-hold Tenancies, there is no right of succession during the fixed term tenancy but it does apply once the fixed term has expired.

HOW TO SUCCEED A TENANCY

1. A claim for succession has to be made to the Landlord to decide if they agree and recognize the potential successor as the new tenant.

2. For a joint tenancy, when one person dies the remaining tenant continues as a successor under the old tenancy. A copy of the death certificate needs to be provided, which enables the information to be updated accordingly.

3. The Housing Officer prepares a succession report within a week of receiving the application. The report will decide which of the following recommendations will be made:

   - That the successor is not valid and so refused.

   - That the successor is agreed at the current property.

   - That the successor is agreed but must be rehoused due to under occupation.

4. When succession has been agreed, an Agreement to Terms of Succession form has to be completed by the successor.

5. A Discretionary Succession is made in exceptional circumstances, e.g. where the tenant who dies is already a successor. The Housing Officer/ Manager will have to use their judgment in making recommendations.

ABANDONMENT

All Secured, Assured and Assured Shorthold and Starter tenants are required to give four weeks' notice to their housing providers before moving out of the property. When a tenant moves out of the property without giving any form of notice and fails to hand in the keys of the property, this is known as abandonment.

The tenant has failed to ensure that the property is his/her sole or principal home, thus appropriate action should be taken to gain possession of the property.

A Notice to Quit should be served on the property in person. The Notice served at the property should be in duplicate - one copy posted through the letterbox and the other attached to the front door. A copy of the Notice should be kept in the tenant file with details of the date it was served. The NTQ expires after 28 days, after which the property can be repossessed as long as the tenant does not return back to the property.

If the tenant returns before the expiry of the Notice they have not abandoned and are legally entitled to resume their tenancy, thus no further action should be taken against the tenant.

HOW TO REGAIN POSSESSION OF THE PROPERTY

1. If there has been no contact from the tenant and the NTQ has expired, the property can be repossessed.

2. It is important to take an inventory of any goods inside the property. This should be carried out by two members of staff and both of whom should sign and date the inventory to ensure that it is correct.

3. It is good practice to take photographs to show the condition of the property when it was repossessed. The date and time should be noted.

4. The locks on the property need to be changed and the tenancy terminated in line with the Organisation's procedure.

5. The tenant cannot be given possession of the property once the entire process has been fully carried out.

MUTUAL EXCHANGE

DEFINITION

Mutual Exchange is where two or more existing tenants move into each other's homes. An exchange can be between the same Landlords or with different public or voluntary sector landlords.

Other points include:

1. Assured and Secured tenants have legal rights to Mutual Exchange.

2. In Mutual Exchange, each tenant takes on the tenancy of the property they are moving into.

3. Mutual exchange is solely organized by the tenant.

4. Assured Short-hold tenants do not have the right to exchange.

5. Assured tenants have the right under Section 92 of the Housing Act 1985 to exchange with another secure tenant, or an assured tenant of a registered social landlord or a Charitable Housing Trust, with the landlord's written consent.

6. A Mutual exchange may affect the rights the tenant previously had. This includes the right to pass their tenancy on should they pass away; as well as the right to buy their home.

PROCESSING FOR MUTUAL EXCHANGE

Once the tenant has found the person they desire to exchange with, they need to obtain the consent of their Landlords. This begins the processes which are as follows:

1. The Housing Officer sends out two application forms, one to each of the tenants. There may be a separate form if the exchange is with an external Landlord.

2. This forms need to be returned as soon as possible. When returned, they should be date stamped to confirm the date it was received.

3. By law a decision for Mutual Exchange must be made within 42 days of receiving the application forms.

4. An acknowledgement letter should be sent to both tenants informing them that their application has been received and will be processed with a specified time frame.

5. A letter should be sent to the external Landlord, if the exchange is with another Landlord.

6. An inspection should be carried on the property by the landlord before the exchange goes ahead. This is to highlight any alternations or damage caused to the property by the tenant or the tenant's household. All alternations or damage will need to be made right by the tenant to the landlord's satisfaction before the exchange can be approved.

7. It is good practice to ensure that there is a valid Gas Safety and Electrical Safety certificate for the property before the exchange goes ahead.

8. The application for the mutual exchange will be approved by the landlord of the applicants in line with the organisation's policy. A Deed of Assignment will need to be signed by both parties.

JOINT TENANCY

A Joint Tenancy is when two or more tenants living in a property share the same tenancy agreement. It can be between a married couple or a co-habiting couple. A tenancy with the name of one person is known as a sole tenancy.

There is no change to tenancy type when granting and ending sole and joint tenancies. The tenancy status remains Secure when a previous sole tenancy is replaced by a joint tenancy and when a joint tenancy becomes a sole tenancy as long as there are no gap in the dates. This is also the case with Assured Tenancies.

CHANGING FROM SOLE TO JOINT TENANCY

An existing tenant can apply for joint tenancy on the following grounds:

1. The prospective joint tenants are married.

2. The prospective joint tenants are cohabiting and have lived in the property for the last 12 months.

3. There are no on-going breaches to the tenancy such as rent arrears, anti-social behaviour issues etc.

4. The property is suitable for the prospective joint tenants.

IMPLICATION OF JOINT TENANCY

It is very important that both applicants understand the legal implications of a joint tenancy, particularly if their relationship were to end. This includes:

1. They are both responsible for all arrears and any breach of tenancy - even if they consider the other has caused the breach of tenancy.

2. Action can be taken against either or both tenants to recover the rent arrears.

3. One cannot remove the other without either a court order, or by ending the whole tenancy.

4. Either of them could end the whole tenancy by giving the appropriate legal notice without the other knowing - it is up to the landlord to decide whether to accept this.

5. If they want the tenancy to pass solely to either of them then this ends any future rights of succession for other family or household members.

6. If they live together as if they were husband and wife then they would have rights of occupation, even if only one of them was the tenant.

LODGERS AND SUB-LETTING

A person who is not a member of the tenant's permanent household living at the property and sharing its facilities in return for payment of rent is known as a lodger. While a person who pays rent to have sole use of a room or rooms in the tenant's home, sharing only some of the facilities, is known as a sub-tenant.

Secured Tenants do have a legal right to have lodgers, while written permission from the Landlord needs to be obtained for Assured tenants. Permission has to be obtained to sub-let part of the property from the landlord both for Assured and Secured tenants.

IMPORTANT POINTS

1. Assured tenants have the right to sub-let as long as permission is granted by the landlord. This is governed by the Housing Act 1989 paragraph 15.

2. Under the Housing Act 1985, a Secured tenant has a statutory right to have a lodger whether the landlord has given permission or not.

3. Written consent has to be obtained for Secured tenants to sub-let part of the property. If the whole of the property is sub-let, it is no longer a secure tenancy and cannot become one again even if the sub-letting ends.

4. The sub-tenant has limited security as they have a resident landlord. To force a sub-tenant to leave the property the tenant must serve a Notice to Quit and obtain a possession order in the County Court. This order can only be enforced by a Court Bailiff.

OVERCROWDING

DEFINITION

Overcrowding is when the number of persons in the household is more than the standard requirement. It can either be statutory or in line with the standard set by the Housing Organisation. It is the natural expansion of the family size and it is one of the most common reasons why people request to be moved.

Following are the permitted number of people per household, as used by many organisations:

1. Couples are entitled to one bedroom.

2. Two single adults are entitled to one bedroom.

3. Two children of the same sex under 16 are expected to share a double bedroom.

4. A boy and girl under ten are expected to share a double bedroom.

It is important to check your options with your Housing Provider if you believe your family is overcrowded. Note that if someone chooses to bring other people into their home, they may not be considered as overcrowded.

CAUSES OF OVERCROWDING

The following are the major causes of overcrowding:

1. Children born to, or adopted by the tenant who lives in the property.

2. The tenant becomes a legal guardian to children.

3. A relative who is a non-dependent of the tenant, who has no suitable alternative accommodation and who does not require care moves in.

4. Children of the tenant or tenant's partner, who usually live elsewhere now reside with the tenant permanently.

5. A close family relative who requires care; this care is provided by the tenant and where this family member has no suitable alternative accommodation.

ENDING A TENANCY

INTRODUCTION

A Tenancy can be terminated in a number of ways, but this must be in line with housing law. It is possible for a tenancy to legally still exist even though the tenant no longer resides there. Tenancies need to be ended using legal methods.

WAYS OF ENDING A TENANCY

The main ways of ending a tenancy are as follows:

1. A notice period is given by the tenant in line with their tenancy agreement. At the end of the notice, the tenant moves out of the property, hands back the keys and signs a relinquishment form.

2. The tenancy ends and it is replaced by another tenancy. An example is through transfers.

3. The property exhibits all the signs that it has been abandoned. The landlord serves a Notice to Quit on the property to end the tenancy. The notice period for the NTQ is usually four weeks.

4. The landlord can end the tenancy. All standard and secure tenancies can only be ended through a court order.

5. When a tenant surrenders their tenancy by removing all of their belongings from the property and returning the keys.

A. TENANT GIVES NOTICE

A tenant is required to give at least four weeks' notice in writing to the landlord, specifying the exact date they intend to move out of the property.

1. The landlord needs to be given access to the property during the notice period to inspect the condition of the property.

2. The rent must be paid up the date of the notice period.

B. NOTICE TO QUIT

1. A Notice to quit can be served by either the landlord or the tenant.

2. It cannot be used by the landlord with a tenancy that is Secured, Assured or Assured short-hold.

3. It can be used to end a tenancy that was originally one of these types but where the status no longer applies. This can be used where:

    ❖ A Secure tenant has abandoned the property - the tenancy still exists even if the tenant is not there, but they have given up their secure status by moving out.

    ❖ Where an Assured tenant illegally lets the property. A notice to quit is served on the illegal tenant and a court application is made to repossess the property.

    ❖ Where a tenanted property is taken over by squatters.

4. A Notice to quit is unilateral - a tenant serving a NTQ does not need the landlord's agreement and neither does the landlord need the tenant's agreement.

5. Only one joint tenant partner needs to serve the Notice to Quit. The whole tenancy will end even if the other joint tenant does not agree or even know about the notice.

6. For a notice to quit served by the tenant to be valid, it must:

    • Expire at the end of a period of the tenancy on a day when the rent is due. This means, for a standard weekly tenancy the date stated on the NTQ must be a Monday.

- Be in writing

- Provide at least 28 days notice

7. For a NTQ served by the landlord, it must also state that the landlord:

    - Must get a court order to evict the tenant.

    - Cannot apply for a court order until the tenancy has ended.

    - Must include a statutory form of words advising the tenant of sources of advice.

C. SURRENDER

1. Surrender can be "expressed" as a deed signed by all parties specifying a date when the tenancy will end.

2. This has to be followed by an action that shows that the tenancy has been surrendered. An example is the tenant moving all possessions from the property and returning the keys to the landlord, who agrees to accept them.

3. Any tenancy, whether fixed term or periodic, Secure, Assured, Assured Short-hold, or Statutory, can end through surrender.

4. Surrender requires the agreement of each party to be valid. The landlord has the choice whether to accept the surrender.

5. Ending a joint tenancy by surrender, the joint tenants must both make the offer.

6. Tenancy surrender can be used to end one tenancy of a property and to immediately replace it with a fresh tenancy. Example is a sole tenancy becoming a joint tenancy.

D. COURT ORDER

The landlord can only end a Secure or Assured tenancy by obtaining a Court Order or Possession Order. The landlord would have to:

1. Serve a valid Notice of Seeking Possession, specify one or more Grounds for possession of the order.

2. They also prove to the court that the ground applies.

IMPORTANT POINTS

1. The Housing Act of 1985 specifies the grounds for possession against a Secured Tenant. The Housing Act of 1988, which was amended by 1996 Housing Act, specifies the ground for Assured Tenants.

2 The court order can be absolute or suspended.

3. A possession order for arrears is suspended as long as the arrears are reduced by specified amounts imposed by the court.

4. When the first payment is missed, legally the tenancy has ended although the tenant still lives in the property.

5. An eviction by a court bailiff is required to repossess the property.

TERMINATION OF FIXED PERIOD TENANCY

This is common with Assured Short-hold tenancy, which is for six months. This type of tenancy can be ended by Court Order or Surrender. However, if the tenant remains after the end of the fixed period and the tenancy is not renewed it becomes a statutory periodic tenancy and may continue as this indefinitely.

Chapter Nine

VOID MANAGEMENT

DEFINITION:

Void is the effective management of empty properties with the aim of reducing the period when it is vacant. It is a term used to describe how the Councils and Registered Social Landlords deal with vacant properties to ensure that rent loss is minimized and the most appropriate properties are added to the housing stock in order to meet housing needs. Effective void management is very important for an Organisation to ensure that it maximizes all its income because income lost during the void periods cannot be recovered.

CAUSES OF VOID

1. Poor contractor performance

2. Abandonment

3. Refusals of Offers

4. Lack of nominations

5. Squatters

6. Poor Environment-Estate

7. Poor Communications among staff in turning around the void property.

8. Lack of notice from tenants moving out to their landlords.

9. Lack of Policy/ Procedure to effectively tackle Void.

EFFECT OF VOIDS

1. Loss of Income

2. Poor estate, such as 'broken windows syndrome'

3. Increase in Homelessness

4. Poor Customer Service

5. Performance Indicator will fall

POSSESSION OF EFFECTIVE VOID MANAGEMENT

1. This is to ensure that the properties of Registered Social Landlords and Councils meet acceptable letting standards.

2. It also ensures the most effective use of housing resources to meet the current housing needs.

3. Registered Social Landlords and the Local Authorities are able to achieve "best value" in the use of their resources.

4. To ensure that housing providers provide decent, secure and affordable housing to meet the housing needs of the government.

5. To ensure that the rent loss through void is kept to a minimum.

RECOMMENDATION

The management of Void is a key performance indicator used to measure the performance of Registered Social Landlords and the Local Authority. It is important that Housing Associations and Local

Authorities maximize the use of their available stock through proper stock control. Targets should be set in place as follows:

1. The percentage of homes that is vacant but available for letting should not be more than 2-3% of the total housing stock in management.

2. Moreover, the average time taken to re-let vacant homes (available for letting) should not be more than three to four weeks.

3. Rent losses arising from void and bad debts should not be more than 4% of the total rent receivable.

4. The target set should be reviewed regularly to highlight areas of improvement and the performance benchmarked with other housing providers of similar size.

WHAT CONSTITUTES VOID MANAGEMENT?

The management of void covers a numbers of activities, these activities include:

1. Giving of notice

2. Tenancy termination

3. Inspections of property

4. Identifying rechargeable works and other tenant responsibilities

5. Ordering of works

6. Offering tenancies and arranging viewings

7. Creating tenancies

Good communication structures should be in place between Housing Management, the Maintenance department and the Lettings department in order to have an effective void management system.

GIVING OF NOTICE

It is very important that set procedures are in place with regards to giving notice. It is also necessary that the tenants know the procedure too. Most registered social landlords include it in the tenancy agreement as an obligation of the tenant. Tenants are required to give their landlord 28 days' notice, and if they fail to comply, they should still be made to pay for the period.

TENANCY TERMINATION

A notice of termination should be given in writing to the landlord and a standard form from the landlord should be forwarded to the tenant for completion. They should request for the following details:

1. Actual leaving date
2. Reason for termination
3. Signatures of all parties to the tenancy
4. Details of other occupants in the property
5. A forwarding address
6. Arrangements for a pre-inspection visit

The notice should be acknowledged immediately and it should detail the following:

1. Confirmation of the termination date
2. Where to deliver keys to and by when
3. A reminder with regards to the need to ensure that the account is cleared by the termination date.
4. Clear guidance on the requirement of the property that is being vacated
5. Date for the pre-inspection visit

Appropriate systems should be in place to deal with terminations as a result of abandonment, eviction, death of the tenant, and any other reason.

INSPECTIONS

Properties that are becoming vacant should be inspected by the Housing Officer prior to the tenant moving out. This is known as a Pre-inspection. The main purpose of this inspection is to:

1. Identify any aspect of disrepair which is the responsibility of the tenant.

2. Agree on the general condition of the property on termination.

3. Identify any repairs that are the responsibility of the landlord.

4. Identify any redecoration allowance for the future tenant.

5. Identify any adaptations or special features of the property, to assist in the allocation process.

A more detailed inspection should be carried out by a Surveyor, once the tenant vacates the property. This is known as a post-inspection and its purpose is to identify all repair works required to the property before re-let.

IDENTIFYING RECHARGEABLE WORKS

A copy of the pre-inspection report should be given to the tenant. Moreover, a deadline should be given to the tenant to address all highlighted repair issues. The property needs to be visited just before the tenant moves, to check on the repairs carried out by the tenant. This is to ensure that all highlighted repairs are carried out to acceptable standards.

ORDERING WORK

It is crucial for Registered Social Landlords and Local Authorities to maintain a turnover period of 3-4 weeks on its vacant property. Any repairs to be carried out after vacation of the property should be ordered as soon as the post-inspection has been carried out. New locks need to be ordered and fitted on the property. It is possible for viewings of the property to be organized while minor repairs are being carried out to save time.

OFFERING TENANCIES AND ARRANGING VIEWINGS

The allocation procedure should be implemented once a termination notice has been received from a tenant. Local Authorities and Registered Social Landlords should have a set policy in place for this purpose. Offers of property should be made in writing. Most Council now have a points and bidding system in place where candidates on a points system go and bid for a property of their choice. This is known as Choice Based Lettings. The following information is sent to candidates:

1. Size and type of the property

2. Proposed date of interviewing and viewing

3. Rent charges

4. Named contact for queries

5. Details of documentation to bring along when coming for the viewing.

The prospective tenant, based on the number of points, will be offered the property. They will be interviewed and signed up for the property.

CREATING TENANCIES

When a prospective tenant has viewed and accepted the property, the Housing Officer should arrange for a sign up of the tenancy. It is very important that the details of the Tenancy Agreement be explained to the new tenant. This is the opportunity for landlords to:

1. Highlight the landlord's responsibilities.

2. Highlight tenants obligations and right.

3. Stress the importance of complying with the Tenancy Agreement.

4. Highlight the consequences of a breach to the Tenancy Agreement.

5. Provide information to the tenant regarding the services provided in the area.

6. Provide the tenant with useful telephone numbers and contact details.

VOID CONTROL

Registered Social Landlords and Local Authorities should have overall control of its void. This is by ensuring:

1. An effective void management procedure and policy is in place.

2. That they have in place reliable Contractors to carryout out void works within a target period.

3. A performance monitoring system is in place. The following performance measure can be used:

    - The number of properties re-let in 2-4 weeks, and over four weeks.

    - The percentage of properties of all re-lets in the year.

    - Void rent loss as a percentage of gross rent debits.

    - The average void period.

    - That the number of properties refused can be no more than two, with good reason.

ENDNOTES

(1) http://www.homesandcommunities.co.uk/
(2) "Housing Association homes" GOV.UK Retrieved 19 December 2012.
(3) Affordable Housing Capital Funding Guide 2012-13.
(4) https://www.gov.uk/definitions-of-general-housing-terms.
(5) www.privatehousinginformation.co.uk/site/123asp
(6) https://www.gov.uk/universal-credit
(7) www.justice.gov.uk/courts/procedure-rules/civil/protocol/prot_rent
(8) www.justice.gov.uk/courts/procedure-rules/civil/protocol/prot_rent
(9) www.legislation.gov.uk/ukpga/1985/68/schedule/2
(10) www.legislation.gov.uk/ukpga/2008/17
(11) www.civilmediation.org/about-mediation/29/
(12) https://www.gov.uk/government/publications/anti-social-behahaviour-crime-and-policing-bill-anti-social-behaviour
(13) Uk.practicallaw.com/A34661-73K
(14) www.legislation.gov.uk/ukpga/1990/43/contents-243k
(15) www.legislation.gov.uk/ukga/1988/50/section/113

INDEX

Abandoned vehicles, 33, 35
Abandonment, 77, 121, 135, 139
abuse, 11
accommodation, 1, 10–11, 43, 45–46, 118, 129
  temporary, 3
  under-occupied, 119
accountability, 42, 85–86
accumulations, 111–12
action plan, 87, 98, 113
Action Planning, 21, 24
affirmation, 74
agencies, 59–60, 62–63, 82, 87, 89
agreement, 3–4, 17, 42, 59, 63, 67, 72–73, 84–86, 88–89, 96, 103, 114–15, 120, 132
  informal, 84
allocation options, 44
allocation procedure, 141
alternations, 124
annoyance, 98
Anti Social Behaviour, 81
Anti-social Behaviour Injunction (ASBI), 98–99
applicants, new, 43–44
arrears, classifying Housing Benefit, 53
arrears agreement, 65, 68
arrears procedures, 64
arrears repayment, 62

Arrest, 105
ASBOs (Anti-Social Behaviour Orders), 86, 89, 97–99
assessment, 16, 21–23, 26, 50
assignee, 115–16
assignment, 115–17, 124
Assured Short-hold, 123, 132–33
Assured Short-hold and Starter tenancies, 116
Assured Short-hold Tenancies, 3–4, 64, 120
Assured Tenancies, 64, 69, 73, 118, 125
Assured tenants, 116, 123, 127, 131, 133
authority, 66, 112

Bailiff Warrant, 75
barrister, 70–71
behaviour, 36, 81, 84, 97, 99, 103
Behaviour Contracts, 86–88, 90
benefits, 1, 55, 59, 61, 66
  claiming,

care, customer, 37, 42
Care Plan, 20, 25–26
care services, 6
  long-term, 20

145

Caretakers, 33–34, 37, 83
Children's Act, 116
Civil Evidence Act, 101
claimant, 56, 73, 79, 107, 109
client, vulnerable, 69
client groups, 9, 12, 20
collusion, 18
commitment, 29, 84, 90, 92
communities, sustainable local, 43
community care, 10
complainant, 84, 87, 98–101, 113–14
complaints procedure, 17
comply, 59, 62–63, 103, 112, 138
confidentiality, 15–16, 18, 21
consent, 35, 123, 127
  landlord's, 117
consolidate, 56
consultation, 27–28, 47, 49
contract, parental responsibility, 88
contractual rights, 116
control, 27, 29, 55, 142
conversions, 47–48
conviction, 90, 110
councils, 27–28, 31, 88, 103, 112, 136, 141
County Courts, 70, 72, 99, 107, 127
court, magistrate, 90, 92, 97
court action, 50, 61–63, 66, 85
court application, 66–67, 131
court hearings, 63, 68–69, 72, 106
Court of Appeal, 73
court order, 72, 79, 103, 116, 126, 130, 132–33
court process, 4
Crime and Disorder Partnerships, 87
Crime Prevention Injunction, 98

Criminal Justice and Public Order Act, 110
Criminal Prosecution and Civil Injunction, 106

Damages, 36, 82, 106, 124
date, termination, 139
debit, direct, 57, 59
Decanting, 47
decants
  permanent, 47–51
  temporary, 47
DECLARATION, 90, 92
Direct Applications, 44
Discretionary Succession, 120
dispute, 94–96, 106
disrepair claim, potential, 66
distress, 81, 90, 92, 97, 105
District Judges, 70
disturbance allowance, 48, 50

Effective void management, 135–36
Employment and Support Allowance, 55
enjoyment, 81, 111–12
Estate Agreement, 38, 42
Estate-based staff, 34, 37
Estate Forums, 31
Estate Inspection Form, 35
Estate Inspections, 33, 37, 39, 41
Estate Management, 5, 27, 33
Estate Services Officers, 83
evict, 75, 132
evictions, 7, 76–77, 133, 139
external agencies, 36, 59, 63

FIXED PERIOD TENANCY, 133
fixed term tenancy, 120
floating support, 7, 99
former tenant, 73, 76–77, 79–80
FORMER TENANT ARREARS, 80
FORWARDING ADDRESS, 78–79

Garnishee Order, 79
Government's Housing Strategy, 43
grant, 4, 69, 117–18
ground
  discretionary, 69
  mandatory, 69, 72

harassment
  cause, 81, 90, 92
  racial, 82, 97
  sexual, 46, 95
Harassment Act, 105, 110
harm, 99, 103, 105, 110
homeless people, single, 12–14
Homes and Communities Agency (HCA), 1–2, 118
housing, social, 3, 98
Housing Act, 1, 3–4, 27, 68–70, 72, 104–5, 119, 123, 127, 133
Housing Associations, 1–5, 27, 43, 47, 56, 65, 97–98, 116, 136
Housing Benefit, claiming, 49, 62
Housing Benefit Arrears, 53
Housing Corporation, 1–2, 10
Housing Managers, 33, 37–38, 42, 49–51, 83
housing matters, 5, 13
Housing Officer, 34, 50, 63, 67, 83, 113, 120, 123, 139, 141

Housing Organisation, 128
housing providers, 4–5, 28–29, 42–43, 46–47, 59–60, 109, 121, 128, 136–37
housing services, 12
housing stock, 7, 135
Human Rights Act Article, 111–12

Imprisonment, 90, 97, 105, 110
Income Support, 55
Injunctions, 98, 104–5
Inspections of property, 138
Intensive Housing Management, 12–13
interference, unreasonable, 111–12
intimidation, 110
Introductory Tenancies, 103
inventory, 34, 121
IPNA, 98–99

Joint tenancy, 118–20, 125, 132
joint tenants, 103, 115, 131–32
judgment debt, 72–73

keyworker, 15–16, 18–19, 22, 24
KEYWORKER SYSTEM, 15
knowledge, 20, 27, 29, 63, 107, 110

landlord
  direct, 116
  external, 123–24
  resident, 127
landlord's responsibilities, 141

legal action, 60, 63–64, 66–67, 79, 83–84, 106, 113–14
LEGAL BACKGROUND, 119
legal interest, 115–16
legal procedures, 66, 94
License, 64–65
Local Authorities and Housing providers work, 63

Magistrates Court, 111–12
maintenance, 6–7, 56
maintenance works, 47–48
Management Agreement, 5, 68
Management Committees, 2
management process, 37
management transfer, 77
mediation, 82, 86–87, 94, 96
Mediators, 95–96
model, 7, 107, 109
monitor, 36, 61, 88, 100
move-on support, 7
Mutual Exchange, 44, 46, 116, 123–24

Neighbourhood Agreement, 31
noise, 82, 85, 112–13
  excessive, 111–12
NOISE ACT, 111–12
Non-legal action, 83
non-tenant, 106
NOSP, 65–66, 68
NTQ, 121, 130–32
nuisance, 81, 84, 98, 104, 111–12

obligation, 45–46, 69, 99, 138
occupants, 2, 103, 112, 139
offence, 110, 112
order
  injunction, 104
  intervention, 98
  suspended, 101, 103
OVERCROWDING, 45, 128
overpayments, 55

PARENTAL CONTROL AGREEMENT, 92
participation, 5, 16, 27, 42
parties, working, 31
partners, 90, 92, 116, 119
partnership, 38, 42–43
payments, 48–50, 54, 62, 65–66, 133
  home loss, 50
  service charges, 53
permission, 28, 86, 96, 127
perpetrators, 84, 87, 99, 101, 103, 105
  alleged, 113–14
  racist, 97
personal circumstances, 3
Personal development, 58
Police Officers, 83, 89, 91, 93
possession order, 69, 71, 73, 117, 127, 133
possession proceedings, residential, 72
post-inspection, 140
Postponed Possession Orders, 73
Power of Arrest, 105
practice, good, 102, 121, 124
Pre-Action Protocol for Rent Arrears, 61

pre-inspection, 139
premises, 3, 34, 73, 111–12
Private Landlord, 65
proceedings, 66, 70, 72, 88–89, 110–12
  civil, 110
  legal, 69
property
  empty, 135
  tenanted, 46–47, 131
  vacant, 43, 135, 140
protocol, 61, 63
  pre-action, 60, 63, 65

Refurbishment, 46, 48
Registered Providers, 2
Registered Social Landlords, 2, 61, 118, 123, 136, 138
re-house, 46, 48
re-lets, 140, 142
rent account, 49–50, 65, 117
  personal, 55
rent arrears, 53, 57, 59–63, 65, 75, 77, 125–26
  eligible, 80
  preventing, 60
Rent Arrears Control, 27, 53, 60
rent arrears policy, 60, 65
rent card, 49, 57
rent liability, 55, 103
rent losses, 135–37
RENT MONITORING PROCESS, 65
RENT OFFICER, 59
rent statement, 67–68
repairs, 6–7, 33, 35–36, 47, 56, 140
  minor, 140
repair works, 46, 49, 140
repayment agreement, 63, 74
repossess, 131, 133
residents meeting, 42
resident's representatives, 42
resources, 24, 29, 94, 136
review, 20–21, 25, 29, 59, 88
risk, 12, 16, 24, 48, 67, 95, 99, 105
risk assessment, 99

Schemes, 10–11, 37
Secrecy, 18
Secured Tenancies, 64, 68, 73
Secured Tenants, 119, 127, 133
service charges, 2, 54
Service Level Agreement, 35, 61
service plan, 20
services
  cleaning, 33–34
  mediation, 96
  welfare rights, 13
service standards, 34–35
set goals, 23, 26
SHORTHOLD TENANCY, 4
SIGN UPS, 84
social landlords, 2, 28, 34–36, 42, 44, 56, 60–61, 83, 105, 109, 118
Social Landlords Crime and Nuisance Group, 105
Social Services, 53, 59
squatters, 131, 135
Statutory nuisance, 111–12
Statutory periodic tenancy, 133
Sub-let, 127
Sub-Tenancy, 65

Sub-Tenancy Agreement, 64
succession, 118–20, 126
successor, 118–20
   qualified, 119
   would-be, 116
Support Agencies, 83
Support Allowance, 55
supported housing, 7–12
supported housing projects, 10
Supported housing providers, 12
support orders, individual, 98
support service delivery, 56
surrender, 132–33
Suspended Possession Orders, 72–73, 75

Tenancy
   existing, 50
   introductory, 103
   new, 50
   probationary, 103
   sole, 119, 125, 132
Tenancy agreement, original, 68, 116
Tenancy Matters, 115
Tenancy Matters and Void Management, 27
tenancy support, 59
tenancy surrender, 132
tenancy termination, 138
Tenant Association, 31
tenant consultation, 5
tenant disputes, 5
tenant file, 121
tenant involvement, 7
Tenant Meetings, 28, 31
Tenant Newsletters, 28

Tenant Participation, 27, 29, 31
tenant relationship, 9, 116
tenant representatives, 2, 31
tenant responsibilities, 138
tenants
   existing, 125
   illegal, 131
   outgoing, 117
   prospective, 86, 99, 141
   sole, 115, 119
   vulnerable, 59
Tenant Services Authority, 1
tenants move, existing, 46, 123
tenant's recommendation, 29
tenant's rights, 99
tenant's spouse, deceased, 119
tenants transfer, 99
termination, 133, 138–41
third party, 18, 78, 110
tools, 34–35, 37, 42, 61, 86, 97
transfers, 5, 7, 44, 46, 103, 115–17, 130
   existing property, 118
trespasser, tolerated, 73
trial possession claims, 101

Under-occupation, 45–46
underpayments, 54
Universal Credit, 55–56
Universal Credit System, 55
usher, 70, 74

Vacant, 135, 137, 139
Verbal agreements, 96
victims, 82, 99, 112

viewings, 138, 140–41
violence, 11, 81, 95
Void Management, 135, 138

Warrant of Possession, 73, 76
welfare, young person's, 89

witness, 101, 110, 117
  hearsay, 101
WITNESS INTIMIDATION, 110
witness statements, 105–8
  supporting, 75

Printed in Great Britain
by Amazon